THE LEGEND OF BLUEBELL FOREST

BOOK ONE

BY ISABELLE DIBB

Illustrations by Jessica Clark
Cover Illustration by Jessica Clark
Cover Design by Melanie Brustad

goodandbeautiful.com

CONTENTS

CHAPTER 1

Glad to be out of the bustling village, Evelyn hurried home on the well-worn path through the woods. The water of the shaded river sparkled through the trees, and she could already hear her family's mill, though it was still a couple of minutes downstream. *Splish, splish.* Evelyn loved the soothing, fluttering sound the waterwheel's wooden slats made as they dipped into and then lifted out of the river.

A rabbit rustled in the thick carpet of bluebells that the forest was named for, and a squirrel with a big, fluffy tail ran down a mossy tree trunk.

From her pocket Evelyn pulled some crumbs left over from her daily delivery of bread rolls to the inn. Each day, she carefully collected the crumbs from the bottom of the basket. She loved watching the woodland animals cautiously creep from their cover in the trees and bluebells, then relax as they munched the tasty morsels. She scattered the crumbs on the path and watched to see whether an animal would come to get them.

While she waited, Evelyn sat down on a rock to catch her breath. Tired from carrying the heavy basket now filled with vegetables purchased at the market, she was glad to pause and appreciate the soft language of the woods. Even with countless birds singing and all the creatures going about their business, Bluebell Forest was still much quieter than the village, with its hurry and commotion.

Suddenly, a shrill animal cry rang through the forest. Evelyn quickly glanced around,

trying to gauge where the sound was coming from. The cry came again, closer this time. Alarmed, she looked up to see a bird spiraling downward—coming right toward her!

On one of its outstretched wings, several feathers were sticking out in odd directions. The bird was clearly in distress. With a final sad call, it plummeted into a tree and lay limply on one of the twisting boughs.

Ignoring the rough bark scratching her hands, Evelyn deftly pulled herself into the tree's branches.

With nimble movements, she soon reached the bird, but was careful to keep her distance, not wanting to frighten the injured creature that lay in a helpless heap.

"It's a pigeon," she whispered, studying its soft gray body and the shiny green patch of feathers on its neck. "Don't be afraid," Evelyn cooed.

Curious, the pigeon stretched its neck out

toward Evelyn. "What's your name?" the girl asked, reaching out and cautiously stroking the bird. She thought for a minute, then decided, "I think I'll call you Pam."

From a nearby tree came a sound she had never before heard in the forest: tinkling bells. Surprised, Evelyn looked up and drew in a sharp breath.

A golden-colored falcon was perched on the limb of a nearby tree, its keen eyes fixed on her and the pigeon. Its sharp beak was hooked like one of the gleaming sickles the farmers used to harvest grain. Evelyn got the feeling that this fierce-looking falcon had been the cause of poor Pam's pain.

The falcon took a step forward, revealing a cluster of bells secured to its foot with a bit of leather.

Quickly, Evelyn picked up the soft, trembling pigeon and cupped it protectively in her hands. It was lighter than she expected for its size. Evelyn was more surprised, though, to feel something stiff and smooth on one of its legs—a tiny scroll of paper.

Her mind burning with curiosity, Evelyn swiftly snapped the thin thread that attached the paper to the bird's leg. The paper was so tightly rolled that it was only the size of Evelyn's little finger. *This must be a carrier pigeon!* she thought in excitement. *I've read stories of pigeons flying long distances to deliver notes, but we've never had any birds that could do that in this area. What could the message be?*

Evelyn started to unroll the paper but was interrupted by a whistle sounding through the woods.

Much to her relief, the falcon turned its piercing gaze from Evelyn and Pam. It gracefully extended its wings and lofted itself into the air.

Hearing footsteps, Evelyn stuffed the tiny

paper into her pocket. A moment later, a boy came walking up the path. The large bird glided toward him and landed on his leather-gloved hand.

The boy appeared to be several years older than Evelyn, had blond hair, and wore an unusual dark blue jacket. Placing a small leather hood on the falcon, he took a startled step back when he caught a glimpse of Evelyn up in the tree.

"Hello. Are you all right up there?" he called.

"Yes, I'm fine, but this pigeon isn't. Your falcon attacked it!"

Cradling Pam gently against the front of her dress, Evelyn climbed down from the tree as the boy came forward to give her a hand.

He looked apologetic but shrugged and said, "Well, he is a hunting bird." Despite his words, a warm blush spread across his cheeks. "I didn't mean for this to happen. I was just taking him out to get some exercise. Truly, I didn't think he would hurt anything."

"But look at this pigeon. Its wing is bleeding!"

The boy stepped forward to take a closer look at the injured bird. He suddenly raised his eyebrows. His eyes darted to the ground, scanning the forest floor. "Did it have a message on it?" he asked.

"Is this your pigeon?" Evelyn questioned, arching an eyebrow.

The boy hesitated and tilted his head. "Well, no . . . it's not. But was there a message on it?"

"A message?" Evelyn asked. *How would he know about the message? Could he have seen the little roll of paper on its leg while it was up in the sky?* Not wanting to let the note fall into the wrong hands, Evelyn asked, "Why does it matter so much if the pigeon isn't yours?"

"It doesn't matter," the boy replied, growing antsy. "But I can bring the pigeon home and take care of it."

"No, no, I insist," Evelyn responded quickly. She was eager to get a chance to help any creature, but she also didn't want this sweet bird to end up near the sharp-eyed falcon. "I found it, and I have lots of practice nursing animals. If I have any questions, I'll ask one of the neighboring farmers, who've taught me most of what I know about caring for various creatures."

"Does your family not farm?" the boy asked curiously.

"No, we operate a mill on the river that flows through Bluebell Forest. People come from the village and countryside to grind their grain. The mill makes flour for our bakery, too," Evelyn explained.

"Oh, do you live at Laughing Pipes Mill?" the boy asked, looking down at his falcon as he stroked its dark feathers.

Evelyn's brow furrowed. "No. I live at Misty Creek Mill. I've never heard of Laughing Pipes Mill."

"What do you mean?" the boy asked, looking confused. "Laughing Pipes Mill has been in this valley for over four hundred years, hasn't it?"

"Our mill is named Misty Creek Mill," Evelyn stated again. "It has been here for over four hundred years. I assure you that there is no other mill in this valley, and I've never heard of Laughing Pipes Mill."

"But—" The boy stopped short, his blue eyes locked with Evelyn's green ones. It seemed as if he wanted to say much more but then changed his mind. He looked away from Evelyn's intense gaze. "Well, that's neat that you have a bakery. I haven't been to the village yet to buy anything. What kinds of pastries do you make?"

"We sell only a few types of bread and rolls, not any pastries. But our bakery is actually at our home out here in the forest. I only go into the village to make deliveries. My mother used to do it, but she has been very sick for a couple of years. Where are you from?"

The boy straightened out the leather straps on the falcon and removed its hood. "Not here, but I'm staying nearby." Then, looking up at the sun climbing higher in the sky, he said, "I should be getting home. Have a good day!"

Turning back in the direction he came from, the boy strode along the path, and the falcon took to the air and soared ahead of him. Evelyn suddenly realized she had never asked the boy's name. He had already disappeared around a bend in the path, but she called out, "Wait! Who are you?"

The boy didn't come back. Maybe he was too far away to hear her, but Evelyn didn't think so. *Is he ignoring me on purpose?* she wondered.

As she pulled out a little twig tangled in her long dark brown hair, Evelyn pondered the interaction. *I know everyone in the valley, and I haven't heard of any newcomers. Maybe this boy is staying with a relative. But why is he sure that there is a mill in this area named Laughing Pipes Mill? And why did he seem to know something about the message on the pigeon?*

I have some questions for him if I should ever meet him again, Evelyn thought with a smile as she looked down at the pigeon. The bird reminded her of the message in her pocket, but home was so close. *And*, she thought, *the boy could still be nearby. I'll wait a little longer to open it.*

She cradled Pam against her with one arm and used the other to heft the loaded basket as she started running, gently but swiftly, her skirt swishing the bluebells beside the path as she went.

CHAPTER 2

Nestled inside a ring of tall cypress trees was the stone cottage where Evelyn's family lived. The house was a hundred years old, but the mill was even older—one of the oldest buildings in the kingdom, except for the castle. Her father always worked hard to keep the cottage and mill in impeccable condition.

As Evelyn neared the house, she saw her papa standing by the path to the cottage, talking with Russell, a farmer who lived nearby. Evelyn waved to the two men, and they smiled back.

Telling them about the message in her pocket

felt important enough to interrupt their discussion, but Evelyn knew doing so would be impolite. Again she thought, *I'll wait.* As she approached the two men, she was puzzled by their conversation.

"So it's just the two cows and the chickens?" Russell was asking.

"Yes," confirmed Papa. "If you still have time, we'll go over to the mill."

"Of course. I have to admit, I've been bringing my wheat here all these years, but I have no idea how to work it."

Papa chuckled and started to reply, but Evelyn didn't hear any more. She was bursting to tell someone about her message, so she ran on.

Evelyn could hear her sister, Alicia, and two brothers, Jacob and Will, playing behind the house, but she was too excited to stop and join their play. Instead, she continued across the clover lawn and into the house.

Quietly taking off her shoes and setting her big basket in the kitchen, Evelyn carried Pam over to her parents' bedroom.

Mama was propped on a stack of pillows and motioned Evelyn in. "You're glowing," said Mama when she saw the huge smile Evelyn wore.

"You won't believe it! I was on my way home when this injured pigeon fell from the sky above me! I think it might have been attacked by a falcon. Meet Pam." Evelyn displayed the pigeon, who rested calmly on the girl's hands yet kept turning her head to look at everything in the room.

"She is so pretty with those shiny green

feathers," Mama admired, but then she furrowed her brow in thought. "Falcons aren't usually allowed in Bluebell Forest. Except for the few houses and their farmyards, most of the land in the forest belongs to the kingdom, so only the royal family can give people permission to hunt here."

"Hmm. I don't know much about falcons, but the boy who had it said he was taking it out for exercise. Maybe that's acceptable if he didn't intend for the bird to hunt anything?" Evelyn responded as she tucked a soft blanket inside a small crate and placed the injured bird on it gently.

A small frown creased Mama's brow as she said, "Possibly." Then her face brightened. "What will you do with the pigeon?" she asked.

"I'm going to help her recover. Her wing is hurt, you see. But then I'm going to release her because look . . ." Evelyn began, pulling the pigeon's message from her pocket and holding it out. "I have no idea why someone would send this. But I'm so curious, and I want to make sure it reaches its owner."

Mama was as excited as Evelyn. "Ooh! A carrier pigeon? I've never heard of a carrier pigeon in this area. What does the message say?"

Evelyn unrolled the small rectangle of paper with her fingertips and then held up the paper as she read the tiny but neatly written words:

"We are now sure that the forest in the legend is Bluebell Forest. We are safe here and will send more information soon."

"What a mysterious message!" Mama declared. "And it's not signed?"

"No," Evelyn replied with a shake of her head. "The boy in the forest also asked me if I lived at—" She suddenly stopped speaking and listened. Mama leaned forward with interest, too. Faintly at first, then louder, the rumbling of wooden wheels on the dirt road sounded from the forest.

"I'll be right back; I'm going to see what's happening!" exclaimed Evelyn.

"Go ahead." Mama chuckled at these words, for Evelyn was already out of the room.

Just as she arrived at the front step, a large wagon came into view. It turned toward the cottage and passed through the opening in the low stone fence that surrounded the front of their property.

Reuben, the son of the village innkeeper, drove the wagon. Boxes and crates were piled inside, and tufts of brightly colored quilts peeped out from between the slats of the crates.

Reuben halted the horses on the swath of clover in front of the house, then slid from the high driver's seat. He rumpled his bright reddish-orange hair, which was already sticking out in all directions.

"Hello," Evelyn greeted him. "What brings you here today?"

"When the stagecoach stopped by the inn a little while ago, one of the passengers got off and needed a ride up to your mill. I figured since I was bringing the wagon anyway, I would give her a ride. I thought you'd already know someone was coming."

A look of surprise crossed Evelyn's face. She had no idea someone was coming to visit or that her family was borrowing Reuben's wagon. *That is a lot of luggage for one visitor*, she thought. *Will all those things even fit in our house?*

Evelyn looked again at the wagon. Half-hidden by luggage, a woman with a thick braid of gray hair sat on the seat inside, searching for something in her handbag. Evelyn definitely didn't recognize her.

The woman looked up and caught the girl's gaze. "Hello! You must be Evelyn."

"Yes, I am," Evelyn responded. She was about to ask the visitor's name when Papa walked into the yard. He wiped the sweat from his forehead with his arm as he noticed Evelyn's questioning glance at the wagon. His flour-dusted sleeve left a white smear across his face.

"Aunt Nora, welcome!" Papa warmly greeted the woman. "You must be so hot and tired from your journey. Evelyn can get you some cold water and a bite of food, if you'd like, while the boys and I unpack the wagon."

"Thank you very much, Andrew, but I'm fine for now," Nora said cheerily. "I'll stay out here to make sure everything gets unloaded all right."

"Of course! Whatever you'd prefer," Papa agreed.

Reuben helped Nora from the wagon and started piling boxes by the door of the cottage. Evelyn assisted, too, picking up smaller boxes, but each one seemed very heavy for its size.

Her sister and two brothers came running into the yard.

"I can help," offered Jacob, the next oldest after Evelyn. He climbed onto the wagon and reached for a large, flat package.

Nora looked skeptically at his muddy hands and knees. "I'm not sure you can lift that . . . " their aunt began nervously.

"Oh, it's all right; I'm ten years old and very strong." Jacob tugged the box down, his arms straining to keep from dropping it. He stumbled a bit as he jumped down from the wagon.

Between the chatter, thumping of boxes on the ground, and snuffling of the horses, the yard was quite chaotic as the family energetically unloaded the wagon. When the task was finished, Reuben waved his goodbyes and started back toward the village on foot, leaving the wagon and horse behind for the family to borrow.

Even Mama, sick as she was, managed to come to the front step and greet their guest. "It's so good to see you, Aunt Nora," she said with a smile, gripping the doorway. Seeing her up and about for the first time in several days, Evelyn's three younger siblings swarmed to Mama like bees clustering around a flower. She wrapped them all in a big hug.

"I'm glad to see you, too, though I'm sorry to see you so unwell," Nora said. "I had no idea until I got Andrew's letter. Hopefully the other doctor will be able to give you the help you need."

Evelyn had not heard anything about this, either. "Is there another doctor around here besides Doctor Dixon?" she asked curiously.

Papa set his hand gently on Evelyn's shoulder. "No, there isn't. It's time we tell you. We made a decision last week." He sighed. "We are going on a journey . . . a long journey."

CHAPTER 3

For a moment, the four children were stunned.

Alicia, who was only six, was the first to speak. "A journey? To where?"

Mama explained, "Last week, Doctor Dixon told me and Papa that he didn't know what else to do for me. But there is a specialist in the kingdom of Heartwood who knows about new types of medicines for my condition and will probably be able to help me."

"The kingdom of Heartwood?" Evelyn gasped. "But there is such a dispute going on between the kingdoms right now. You told us that Heartwood is threatening to cut off trade between our kingdoms and close its borders."

"That's right," Papa agreed, "and that's even more of a reason why we need to go immediately. Mama has to see the doctor, but if Heartwood closes its borders, she won't get the help she needs. Maybe the shutdown is just a threat, but I don't want to risk it. This is our only hope to help your mother get well. Everything is going to be all right."

Even though Evelyn was concerned about Mama, her heart fluttered with excitement at the thought of traveling somewhere so far away. She had never gone very far from the village and the vast stretches of farmland that surrounded it, and now she would get a chance to go to another kingdom! What adventures awaited their family?

"The doctor said it was urgent to go, so we are leaving as soon as possible," Papa explained.

"We were waiting to tell you till Aunt Nora came since we weren't sure if she could make it, but everything is arranged now." He continued, "I have rented this wagon from the innkeeper, and all that's left to do is pack what we will need for the journey."

"What about the bakery? And the mill? Where else will people in the village grind their grain or buy bread?" eight-year-old Will asked.

"That's why I'm here," Nora chimed in good-naturedly. "Your papa invited me to stay here for a little while and keep the bakery running."

Papa continued, "I've arranged with Russell, our friend and neighbor, to work the mill a couple of days each week and check on our animals now and then to make sure they are staying healthy. Evelyn will be able to feed the chickens and cows, but Russell will be here if you need anything else."

The smile on Evelyn's face faded as her heart sank. She asked, "So I won't be coming along?"

Papa took a deep breath and wove his fingers together. "No, I knew you would want to go, but Nora will need your help here. It would be a lot for her to take care of the younger children, so we are taking them with us, but she will need someone to help with the work of the bakery."

I don't know Aunt Nora at all, Evelyn thought with concern, *and now I won't have the chance to travel. But even worse, I won't know what's happening to Mama!*

Little Alicia frowned. "I'll miss Evelyn. We can't leave her here!"

Papa sighed. "I'll miss her, too. We all will. But we will write her lots of letters."

"And you can send us letters, too," Mama told Evelyn, who was frozen in place. She was still turning all of this news over in her mind and trying to decide what to think and how she felt.

Thrilled by the prospect of the journey, Jacob asked, "What do we need to get ready?"

"We need to pack clothes for everyone," Papa replied. "And I have a list of food and other supplies for Mama and me to gather. We expect to be gone for around five or six weeks, depending on how quickly we can travel and what sort of treatment the doctor prescribes."

Evelyn couldn't believe what she was hearing. *Five or six WEEKS?! That is such a long time!*

Evelyn's siblings went into the cottage, chattering and eager to gather their belongings for the journey. Nora also went inside, carrying her handbag and an oddly shaped straw hat.

But Evelyn stayed with her parents. "How come I have never met Aunt Nora?" Evelyn asked, wondering both why her aunt hadn't come to visit before and how she would now be able to stay for such a duration.

"For a long time, she lived in faraway mountains," Papa explained, "but Aunt Nora lived with my family for a couple of years when I was younger. I've kept in touch with her; we sometimes send each other letters. Since her husband died a few years ago, she has been staying with different friends, but she doesn't have a home to call her own. I didn't think this house would be big enough for her to be comfortable staying here with all of us, but we might be able to work out a way for her to stay when we get back from our trip."

"Evy, I know you wish you could come with us, and this is all very sudden," Mama said. "But I don't think the bakery can survive without someone who knows all the ins and outs of running it like you do. Aunt Nora can make bread, but she has never worked at a bakery or mill. You are so skilled, and our customers trust you. We need you to stay and help Aunt Nora keep things running until we get back."

Evelyn wanted to protest, *I'm only thirteen years old! I can't do all of that!*

Papa seemed to read her thoughts. He wrapped her in a warm hug. "Aunt Nora will help you, and so will God. Before you know it, we'll be back, and Mama will be healthy at last."

Letting out a sigh, Evelyn nodded. "You're right. I'll stay and help so Mama can get well."

Mama gave Evelyn a long hug, squeezing as tightly as she was able. "Now, you should attend to the hurt bird," Mama reminded her, knowing it would take Evelyn's mind off the coming changes.

Soon Evelyn was bandaging Pam's hurt wing and finding old dishes for the bird's food and water.

Over the next hour, the house was filled with activity as the family made the remaining preparations for their departure. Nora started bustling around the kitchen and announced after a little while that lunch was ready. She had whipped up some flaky biscuits and a pot of hearty, silky tomato soup. Conversation around the table soon turned to Pam, and Evelyn retold the story of finding the bird, its message, and the strange boy in the forest.

Papa frowned. "A legend about this forest? I've never heard of Bluebell Forest having a legend."

"What is a legend?" Alicia asked.

"It's a story that has been handed down from the past," Nora explained.

The little girl's curiosity continued. "Is it a true story?"

Papa shook his head. "Legends are not always reliable stories, but they often are based on some part of history."

"Legends often get changed over time," Nora added. "I am a history enthusiast, and I've brought a lot of books along with me." She turned to Evelyn. "I hope you are looking forward to some history lessons. I'm excited to be taking over your schooling and helping out with the farm, too."

A swirl of thoughts entered Evelyn's head as she smiled politely at her aunt. *Schooling? I haven't done much schooling at all since Mama has been sick. But I do love history, so maybe it will be fun.*

Nora continued. "Much of the history of our

kingdom is legend, unfortunately. For reasons that I haven't been able to figure out, we don't have a solid history of our kingdom or our sister kingdom, like many other kingdoms do."

"What's a sister kingdom?" asked Jacob.

"Great question," Nora said, smiling kindly at Jacob. "I haven't heard of it anywhere else. But our kingdom, Heartsong, and the next kingdom over, Heartwood, have been closely connected for as long as anyone can remember. Yes, each kingdom has its own king and queen and government, but the borders have always been wide open for trade, and both kingdoms have very similar governments and laws."

"That seems to be changing," Papa murmured with a frown. He stood and pushed his chair back. "In fact, I feel such an urgency to get through the border to Heartwood that I'm going to finish getting the last things packed up so we can be on our way."

"Wait," Evelyn called out. "Can I ask you a question before you go?"

Papa nodded.

For a moment, Evelyn hesitated, but then she asked, "Have you ever heard of a mill called Laughing Pipes Mill being in this valley? The boy with the falcon thought I lived at a mill with that name."

Papa's brow furrowed. "No, this mill belonged to your great-grandfather, and it was named Misty Creek Mill when he owned it."

"That's what I thought," Evelyn replied. "Thank you, Papa."

As the last few bags were being loaded onto the borrowed wagon, her siblings arranged a nest of blankets to sit on. Evelyn felt trepidation at the thought of being apart from her family, but hope rose within her, too. This was a chance for Mama to be well at last. Even so, Evelyn felt tears fill her eyes and slide down her cheeks as she waved goodbye to her family.

Once the wagon disappeared around the farthest bend in the road, Nora patted her on the shoulder before heading into the house, leaving Evelyn to her thoughts and feelings.

Busying herself in hopes of being distracted from her worries, Evelyn went to the chicken coop to check if there were any eggs. She refilled the chickens' bucket of water while the flock gathered around her, hoping for a scrap from the kitchen as a treat. Since she didn't have anything for them, she leaned down to pet a few of the hens until they lost interest and drifted away, returning to scratching and digging in the dirt for bugs. Hot tears glided over her cheeks as she watched the hens scatter. With three eggs balanced in one hand, she closed the latch to the coop and headed to the house.

Reluctant to let this aunt she barely knew see her crying, Evelyn avoided Nora for most of the evening. The older woman seemed to understand and tactfully let Evelyn have some time to herself. Later, over dinner, Nora told such delightful stories about Papa as a child that Evelyn was comforted, feeling happier and reassured that she would get along with her aunt.

That night, Evelyn stared out the panes of her bedroom window at the canopy of twinkling stars. The night sky always made her feel very small but full of wonder at the same time. A breath of cool night wind sighed through her open window and brushed her cheek, and she snuggled deeper into her colorful patchwork quilt.

Then she heard it: the very faint, hauntingly beautiful music that seemed to be coming from far, far away. She sat up in bed to listen. *It shouldn't surprise me*, Evelyn thought. The music, which she could hear if her window was open, had come around this time two or three nights a week ever since she could remember. A few times, she had even heard the music during the daytime, when she was outside. The melody was not always the same, but it was always a slow-moving tune. No one in the village knew where the melody came from. For decades, people had hiked through the hills searching for the source of the sound, but no one could find anything. The music was so faint, it was impossible to discern the kind of instrument it emanated from.

Evelyn closed her eyes. *Whichever instrument it is, it sure carries far. I wonder if my family can hear it, too.* Before the faint melody ended, she was fast asleep.

CHAPTER 4

Waking up to an unusually quiet house, Evelyn opened her eyes and stretched. The walls of the room were tinted pink with the first brightening of the sky.

Yawning, she saw her younger sister's bed was empty but neatly made. *Where's Alicia?* Evelyn wondered.

Then she remembered: Yesterday after lunch her family had left for the kingdom of Heartwood. Today there would be no clatter from all the children helping Papa measure ingredients in the kitchen or knead dough. Only

Evelyn and Nora were left to attend to all the duties of the house and bakery.

I'll have to make the bread today, she thought. *It won't be the same without Papa's jokes or Mama's singing.*

Then she heard Pam coo from the pigeon's cozy crate in the corner of the room. Nora had said it would be good to have the pigeon where Evelyn could keep an eye on her for a couple of weeks while Pam was regaining strength.

Evelyn hopped out of bed and went over to see how the bird's wing was doing. As she softly stroked the pigeon's back, she examined the place where the feathers had been torn out. While she attended to the bird, she considered what the weeks ahead would hold and thought, *I rather like being responsible and taking care of things. I am excited to see what it's like to run the bakery without Mama or Papa, and I do have someone to help. It will be fun to get to know*

Aunt Nora and to see what she has to teach me about history.

Evelyn went over to the cushioned window seat in the little room and picked up her journal. When she glanced out the window, she saw the sun peeking over the trees, piercing through the grayish fog hovering in the forest. Evelyn sat down and opened the journal.

Suddenly, something warm and furry ran out from behind Evelyn and tumbled onto her lap. Catching a glimpse of its peculiar-looking face, Evelyn let out a high-pitched scream.

As Evelyn leaped up, the creature darted out of the room through the open door. It seemed to be a huge rat—maybe too big to be a rat, but definitely not a dog or cat.

She heard the brisk, light footsteps of Nora in the hall coming to see what was the matter. She appeared in the doorway, concern and surprise on her face. "What has . . ."

"I'm so sorry I screamed," Evelyn said, trembling, "but there was a terrible rodent of some sort that jumped onto my lap!"

Nora relaxed. "Ah, I believe you've met Freddy."

"Who?" asked Evelyn, perplexed. "You . . . own . . . a rat?"

"Ferrets, actually. They aren't rodents at all. I have five, but I normally keep them in their crate so they don't chew on things. Freddy has

always had a longing for adventure, though, and he sometimes gets out."

All Evelyn could think to say was "Oh."

She was not sure she liked the idea of having this strange creature in the house—not to mention five of them! Freddy did not seem very well trained, either. *Maybe I can help with that, though*, she thought, trying to reassure herself.

"Well, should we start making the bread for today?" Evelyn asked.

"Oh, I have that all taken care of," said Nora with a wave of her hand. "All the dough is already rising. Why don't you take care of Pam, milk the cow, and feed the chickens, and then we'll get started with your new schedule."

"Schedule?" A funny feeling entered Evelyn's stomach at the thought of that word. With her mother being so sick for a couple of years, and with her father doing all he could to keep them clothed and fed, there hadn't been much schooling or scheduling in their family life.

Seeing Evelyn's worried expression, Nora laughed and her eyes twinkled. "Don't worry. A schedule is a good thing. You'll see. Now, shoo. Go take care of the animals. I'll have breakfast ready for you when you're done."

Breakfast sounds good, Evelyn thought, her mind turning toward the injured bird in her room. First, Evelyn gave Pam a fresh bowl of water. Then she changed the bandage on the wing.

Next, she milked the cow. As she carried the pail of frothy milk out of the barn, she nearly tripped on a pile of loose, freshly dug dirt. Evelyn steadied the bucket, losing only a splash of the milk. *Who made that pile of dirt right in front of the doorway?* she wondered.

A few minutes later, as she was walking over to the henhouse to tend to the chickens, she noticed a few more piles of dirt around the base of the mill. *Did the ferrets escape or a family of gophers just move in?* Evelyn speculated, puzzled by these piles of dirt.

However, when she went to the mill to get grain to feed the chickens, she saw something that surprised her even more. The huge barrel of grain for the chickens, which stood against the front of the mill, had been pushed several feet to the right.

That's so strange! Evelyn mused, knowing Nora couldn't have shifted the heavy barrel by herself. *I've never seen that barrel moved—not ever. Did Papa move it over before he left? Why would he have done that?* A massive dip in the ground marked where the heavy barrel had sat for years. Evelyn noticed freshly dug dirt around the dent. Then something caught her eye. Evelyn dropped to her knees, not caring that her light green cotton dress and white apron were getting dirty. In the freshly dug indent, a large flat stone had been uncovered. Evelyn carefully brushed off the remaining clusters of dirt, revealing words carved into the ancient-looking rock.

The stone was worn and very dirty. Evelyn placed her finger on the first letter and traced it. “It’s an L,” she said aloud. Hardly breathing, she deciphered letter after letter. Before she was finished, she realized what the letters spelled, and her heart beat quickly. She leaned back on her heels.

“I can’t believe it,” she whispered. “Who uncovered this?”

There was no answer other than the soft clucking of a few chickens nearby, a bird twittering on a branch above her, and the familiar soft *splish, splish* of the waterwheel’s paddles.

Suddenly, a loud screech pierced the air, and Evelyn lifted her face, scanning the sky with her wide green eyes, her long brown hair swirling around her shoulders with the quick turn of her head. The falcon she had seen yesterday circled above her, its leather jesses trailing behind it.

Evelyn started to stand up, intending to run to the cottage. However, she fell back down to the ground as it suddenly rumbled below her. A shingle flew from the low-hanging roof of the mill, landing close to her, and the whole earth vibrated. Evelyn curled in a ball, watching the trees swaying far above her before she closed her eyes. From inside the mill came a deep, tremendous crashing along with the sound of shattering wood.

And then all was still. Too still. The bird that had been twittering had flown away. Even the chickens were quiet.

"Evelyn! Evelyn!" Nora's voice, full of concern, came ringing across the yard.

Blinking away her confusion, Evelyn slowly

rose to her feet. “I’m by the mill!” she called. “I’m safe!”

Before Evelyn had time to brush off her dress and apron and pull some leaves out of her hair, Nora came running.

“I think we just experienced an earthquake!” Nora cried. “Are you absolutely certain you’re not hurt?”

“I—yes, I’m all right,” Evelyn said. “We’ve had a couple of small earthquakes here this year, but nothing like that.”

Both of them sat there for a minute, breathing deeply to calm themselves.

Then Evelyn glanced into the sky and noticed that the falcon was gone. She also remembered what she had just discovered. “Aunt Nora, look!” She pointed to the ground beneath her feet. “Someone has been digging all around the base of the mill, and they’ve uncovered this stone plaque.”

Just as Evelyn had done, Nora dropped to her knees, her thick gray braid swinging over her right shoulder. "This is very old. I can hardly read it. Can you read what it says?" she asked, squinting at the words and gently touching the letters.

Evelyn took a deep breath. "It says, 'Laughing Pipes Mill.'"

CHAPTER 5

Evelyn half expected her aunt to offer some explanation, some answer to the mystery, but Nora was as puzzled as she was. Shaking her head slowly, Nora read the age-worn inscription on the stone to herself. "I lived here for a couple of years long ago, but I am positive I've never heard of Laughing Pipes Mill. Why would this be here?"

"It was called Misty Creek Mill even in my great-grandfather's time," Evelyn agreed. Remembering what the boy with the falcon had said about the mill's name, she asked, "As you've studied the history of the kingdom, have you learned about any mills besides this one that used to exist in this valley?"

"No, none. I wonder why we haven't heard of Laughing Pipes Mill if that was its original name."

From the still forest came a sudden pounding of footsteps. Looking up abruptly, Evelyn saw the boy she had met in the forest, running toward the mill.

He stopped short, his breathing labored, when he saw Evelyn and Nora kneeling beside the mill. Maybe it was only his rapid pace, but he seemed a bit flustered. Before anyone had time to exchange greetings, his swift falcon had arrived, too, and landed on his forearm. "Good morning! What brings you here?" Evelyn asked, her interest piqued.

"I was nearby, exercising my falcon, when I felt the earthquake and then heard a terribly loud crashing sound at the mill. I wanted to make sure everything was all right here. Are you hurt?"

"No, just a little shaken, if you know what I mean," Evelyn replied with a weak laugh. "Thanks for asking."

Noticing Evelyn warily watching the falcon, the boy offered, "I'll have my falcon wait for me in a tree." With a whistling sound, he signaled for the bird to fly up to a branch, and it promptly took wing and headed in the direction the boy indicated.

"Thank you," Evelyn said gratefully. Noticing her aunt's curious glance, she continued, "Aunt Nora, I'd like you to meet . . ." Evelyn paused, remembering she didn't know the boy's name.

"Oliver," he filled in.

"I don't know if I introduced myself, either. My name is Evelyn."

"It's a pleasure to meet you," Oliver responded politely.

"Oliver just moved here—or at least he said he is staying nearby," Evelyn explained. "He owns a falcon, and we met each other when Pam got injured."

"I'm new here as well. Where are you from?" Nora asked Oliver.

Oliver shrugged casually. "Oh, it's very far off. I doubt you would have heard of it."

"I'm sure I have," Nora insisted, putting her hands on her hips. "I'm just about an expert on Heartsong Kingdom—and of Heartwood, too. I know a lot about their history and geography! I truly would like to hear where you're from."

Oliver gazed up into the treetops. After a moment he said, "I lived in Elk Grove."

Nora studied the boy, eyebrows raised. "Hmm. I've never heard of it." A hint of inquiry filled her words.

"Don't worry. It's quite . . . quite a small place," assured Oliver. He exhaled.

He seems to be relieved, Evelyn thought, *and he's behaving rather mysteriously. And he said he didn't know where the bakery was. What was he doing nearby?*

Hesitating, Evelyn pointed to the hole at her feet and asked, "Were you the one who uncovered the plaque?" Her question seemed to make Oliver even more uncomfortable.

All at once, a ponderous creak resounded from within the mill. "What was that mighty crash in the mill earlier?" Oliver questioned with concern. "Was the machinery damaged by the earthquake?"

Evelyn gasped. "I hope not!"

They rushed into the mill, where Evelyn drew in a sharp breath.

One giant millstone remained on the low platform in the center of the mill, its grooved surface exposed. The round stone that usually rested on top and ground grain as it turned by the waterwheel's power lay on the ground. It had slid off its companion, cracking in two and causing the wooden floor to warp and buckle under its enormous weight. With edges sharp and uneven, the halves of the millstone were like a tree split by lightning. Splinters of the wooden floor were strewn about the mill, adding to the scene of destruction.

"Oh no," Evelyn said in a choked whisper. She could tell that her aunt was as shocked as she was. The two stood in silent despair inside the dim mill, dust swirling about them.

"Could you, uh, fix it?" Oliver asked a little awkwardly.

"No," Evelyn replied, her voice wobbly. "Millstones need to be carved from one solid piece of rock, and the right type of rock comes from far away," she explained. "This one has been in the family for—well, I don't even know how long. It's many generations old."

Oliver began to explore the mill, investigating the floor and machinery, but Evelyn remained by Nora. “What will we do without Papa? He’s the only one who knows anything about the mill,” Evelyn whispered tremulously. She felt a tear run down her cheek. “I wish my family hadn’t gone away.”

“Evelyn, they will soon be back,” Nora reassured her. “Your parents will know where to locate someone who sells millstones and be able to get everything back up and running. We can wait until then.”

Evelyn closed her eyes and breathed deeply, listening to the gentle flow of the river. When Evelyn opened her eyes, she saw the bright morning sunlight coming through the open door of the mill, and she smiled a little. “You’re right. Things always have a way of working out,” she finally told Nora.

Looking thoughtful, Nora began to plan.

"Now we won't be able to grind any more grain, so we won't have the income from the mill. And we'll have to shut down the bakery, too, once we run out of flour, at least until we can get a steady supply again."

"But we do have some bags of flour left, probably enough to bake bread and rolls for two or three more weeks," Evelyn estimated.

Nora seemed to be doing some counting in her head. "I brought everything I have with me," she explained, "and I have some savings that could get us through a few more weeks, I believe, but we will have to be frugal."

"Look over here!" Oliver exclaimed. His inspection of the mill had ended near the broken millstone. Pointing to its thick rim, he asked, "Have you ever seen these before?"

Evelyn stepped closer to see what he was talking about. "Those markings? They've always been there."

“Do they mean anything?” Oliver questioned. He touched one and slid his finger along the stone’s curving edge to another faint marking. “Is the whole alphabet on here?”

Evelyn shrugged. “Well, there are a few letters, I’m almost sure, but they’re pretty faint. They don’t go along with anything.” She had never really given them much thought, especially not now, with the greater concern of the broken millstone looming over the mill and bakery.

“But there’s a symbol beneath each letter, too,” Oliver insisted. Slowly and thoroughly, he traced his finger along the edge of the millstone, first one half, then the other.

“All the letters of the alphabet *are* around the stone. Have you never wondered what the symbols mean?”

“Not really. I’ve lived here since I was born, and I grew up seeing the markings. Once,

I tried to decipher them, but I couldn't get anywhere with it. No one knows what they are, as far as I know, so I haven't even thought about them for years."

As Oliver continued to curiously absorb every detail, Evelyn watched him studiously. *He seems excessively interested in the mill*, she mused. She remembered how he had called it Laughing Pipes Mill and had been so eager to find out about the message the pigeon carried. *Could what he said about the mill's name be connected to the legend?* Evelyn wondered.

"Wait," she blurted out. "Oliver, have you ever heard stories about Bluebell Forest? Maybe a legend or something?"

"What do you mean?" he asked without looking up.

Evelyn took a deep breath. "Remember that pigeon in the forest?" Seeing Oliver nod his head, she rushed on. "Well, there actually was a message on the pigeon, but I hadn't read it yet. I was worried it would fall into the wrong hands, and I didn't know you. But the message said something about a legend."

Oliver turned slowly to face her and Nora, thinking. "Would you be willing to show me the message before I explain what I know? It might be helpful for context."

What's the harm? It's such a short message without much information, Evelyn thought. *And Oliver already knows about Laughing Pipes Mill. He was the one who mentioned it in the first place.* "Sure. I'll bring it to you in just a minute."

Oliver stepped outside the mill, and Evelyn walked into the house, Nora following behind her. Evelyn went to her room and grabbed the small note, which was tucked safely in her journal.

When Evelyn entered the kitchen, Nora was

already back at work. "The loaves of bread that were baking in the ovens got flattened by the earthquake," she said, "but I'll let the rest of the dough rise again. The muffins I was making for breakfast are still all right. Here, bring one to Oliver," she urged, holding one of the large, still-warm muffins out to Evelyn. "It's early to be wandering around the forest, and he may not have had breakfast yet."

"I'm sure he'll appreciate that," Evelyn replied as she took the muffin her thoughtful aunt offered. *Yes, it is early. Where could he be staying? There aren't any houses nearby.*

As Evelyn hastened to the door with the message and muffin in her hands, Nora cried, "Wait! Bring another muffin, too. Boys his age are always hungry."

Evelyn giggled and grabbed a second muffin. In the soggy grass, her shoes left a faint trail of footprints on her way through the yard.

When she reached the quiet mill, Evelyn peered around the corner of the building and walked to the other side. She then pulled open the heavy door to look inside.

"Oliver?" Her voice rang through the empty mill.

The boy was gone.

CHAPTER 6

As Evelyn ran back to the cottage, she saw Nora standing outside the front door. "Oliver's gone! He just left without a word!" Evelyn cried. Her aunt's eyebrows flew up.

"He did?" Nora exclaimed, disappointment in her voice. "That's too bad." Drumming her fingers against her embroidered apron, she asked, "Could I have a look at the note? I've heard the message, but I haven't actually seen it yet."

"Of course," Evelyn replied as she handed the small slip of paper to her aunt.

Nora held it up to inspect it more closely. "We are now sure that the forest in the legend is Bluebell Forest. We are safe here and will send more information soon," she read aloud.

Handing the note back to Evelyn, Nora remarked, "Hmm. This is all very mysterious." Then she brightened and turned to go inside. "But for now, we need to focus on all the work before us. Breakfast is ready, so wash up!"

"What do you mean? We've already finished the farm chores and most of the baking!" Evelyn called, but her aunt was already through the doorway.

At the hand pump that stood halfway between the cottage and the barn, Evelyn washed the bits of grass and dirt off her skin with the cool flow of water pumped from the creek. When she stepped into the cottage moments later, a medley of delicious aromas greeted her. The table was set with herb-sprinkled fried eggs, muffins covered in deep pink jam, and steaming mugs of hot chocolate with swirls of fresh cream.

"Oh, thank you, Aunt Nora!" Evelyn exclaimed enthusiastically. The two sat down at the table. Before they said a short prayer of gratitude for the food, Evelyn glanced around at the seats left empty by her traveling family. A pang of sadness twisted in her belly, and she added a quiet prayer for her family's travel and her mother's healing. Then Evelyn bit into a muffin, closing her eyes as she savored its flavors. "What type of jam is this?" Evelyn asked.

"It's rose jam."

"Mmm. I love it. We've always had all the roses we could want in the summer, but I've never thought about eating them!"

"Most people haven't! But I'm famous for my rose jam where I come from. I brought this with me, but I'd like to try making some here."

As Evelyn and Nora ate and chatted, broad shafts of light slanted through the windows into the big kitchen. Once they had finished all the delicious food on their plates, Nora stood up and grabbed something from the counter.

"Well now! It's time to begin with our plans for the day! Here is your schedule." She handed two sheets of paper to Evelyn, who was shocked. She had forgotten all about Nora's plan to make a schedule.

"As you see, we will get our chores done in the morning, and then we will have writing lessons, arithmetic, and literature studies. After lunch, we will have history lessons while we walk to the village to deliver the rolls to the inn."

In a panic, Evelyn looked at the schedule in her hand. Then she flipped to the other sheet of paper and saw a list of chores.

Evelyn frowned, slightly perturbed at this turn of events. She didn't want to hurt Nora's

feelings, though, so she said, "It was kind of you to make a schedule to try to help me. I appreciate the thought. But," she explained, "I hate arithmetic, and there is no need to know any more about numbers than I do already."

Nora put her hands on her hips. "Are you sure? Maybe you just don't understand enough arithmetic yet if you don't like it."

Evelyn shook her head with certainty. "And I haven't had to do writing lessons for nearly two years. I really don't need any better handwriting than I already have," she continued and added silently, *And I don't care to, either.*

Nora's glance flicked skeptically from Evelyn to a recipe the girl had copied that lay on the counter and then back to the girl, unconvinced. *Actually, my handwriting is bordering atrocious*, Evelyn admitted to herself, feeling a tiny twinge of self-reproach.

But she shook her head and continued, "A

history lesson on the walk might be fun, though I normally like to enjoy the forest in silence. I'm used to doing chores, too, but I don't know how to do all the things on this list. And I'm not sure what the subject of literature even entails," she persisted.

Nora listened respectfully with calm attention, then looked directly into Evelyn's eyes. "I can tell this troubles you. Is there anything else?" Nora asked.

"It's too much! We can't fit all of this in a day," Evelyn exclaimed. "I won't have time to do anything I normally do."

Nora gazed out one of the windows and thought for a moment. "Evelyn, I know you wish you could spend all of your days exploring Bluebell Forest, but there are other important things you must do as well. You may think this sounds like a big chore, but I expect that you are going to really enjoy learning. Just wait and see."

Evelyn sighed.

"We will begin with writing lessons," Nora stated, firmly but kindly. "Go get your slate and chalk."

"I'm not even quite sure where it is," Evelyn mumbled as she left the room. She dove under her bed to search for her long-neglected school materials. In the far corner, she found a short, rather crumbly piece of chalk and her slate, with a layer of dust so thick she couldn't see the black through it.

Returning to the kitchen, Evelyn plunked the slate on the table, where it emitted a puff of musty grayish dust.

"No, no, bring that and follow me," Nora told her. Much to Evelyn's surprise, her aunt picked up her spacious handbag and went out the front door! Taking big steps to catch up, Evelyn followed behind with her slate.

Sunlight dappled the leaves quivering in

the warm, gentle breeze as Nora and Evelyn strolled through the forest. They soon reached the sandy bank of the river. Below was the briskly moving blue water, and above was a lush meadow speckled with an array of colors, as if an enormous brush of paint had been flicked over the verdant foliage and left splatters in every hue.

Nora sat down on a moss-covered rock. "There is such a marvelous variety of flowers here. Why don't you gather a bouquet of them?" she suggested, opening a book she had brought in her bag. "Just come back in a couple of minutes."

Evelyn promptly skipped off to the meadow. *It looks like we're not having a writing lesson after all,* she thought with a relieved grin. Pleasantly surprised, she nevertheless wondered why they had come here just when Nora said the schoolwork was going to start.

Scouting around the multicolored meadow, Evelyn plucked buttercups, violets, and various other flowers until she held a vibrant bunch of blossoms.

When Evelyn brought her collection back to her aunt, Nora laid the bundle of flowers on the ground and selected a few.

"Do you know what types of flowers these are?" she asked Evelyn.

"Ooh, I know all of them except this purple one," Evelyn answered proudly.

"That one's columbine. Now, what do you notice about the petals of these flowers?" Nora inquired.

"All the petals are the same, and they are so round and smooth and . . . tiny!"

"I agree! The flowers are perfectly shaped, and all the parts are uniform. Can you imagine what care it must have taken to create these?"

"They are very beautiful," Evelyn agreed.

"Writing can be an art, too," Nora said. "Now I want you to write the name of each flower with as much elegance and uniformity as you can, just like the flowers. And then we will be finished."

That's all? Evelyn thought. "All right. Columbine, aster, sorrel . . ." She recited slowly as she wrote each word, trying her best to focus and make each letter beautiful and shapely. In spite of her aversion to handwriting, a delighted smile crept to her face.

But the writing lesson was interrupted before Evelyn had completed writing all the flowers' names. Hastening along the riverbank was Russell, the broad-shouldered, red-haired neighbor whom Evelyn's father had asked to help with the mill and livestock. His boots left a trail of divots in the sand. "Have you seen the millstone?" he called, his voice laden with dismay.

"Yes," replied Nora, unruffled, as she closed her book.

"Well, I'm glad I'm not the first one to bring you the news. I came to the mill this morning to help out, and I was shocked when I saw the broken stone. I'm so sorry, but there's nothing I can do."

"Don't worry. We will have to make a few changes, but we'll be just fine," Nora assured him.

"Well, I suppose there isn't any more work for me to do here, but I will come by now and then to check on how things are going," Russell offered. "The wooden waterwheel received some damage as well, but that shouldn't be hard to repair. I'll try to get it back to its old spinning self when I have some time. Reach out to me if you need anything."

"We are so grateful that you are looking out for us," Evelyn told him. "Was there any damage at your farm? Is your family all right?"

"Thankfully, none of us were harmed, and neither were any of our livestock. I was in town earlier today and saw a few cracked windows, but everything else there is unscathed. It looks like the mill sustained more damage than anything else."

As she recalled her experience with the earthquake, Evelyn thought of Oliver. "Russell," she asked, "have you seen a boy around here who isn't from Bluebell Forest? He's a few years older than I am, and his name is Oliver."

Russell clasped his hands and thought for a moment. "Now that I think of it, I did, actually. I saw a boy with blond hair walking up the hill on the other side of the valley yesterday, and there was a girl with him who looked a little older than he was. I don't know anything about them, though."

"Thank you," Evelyn said. "I was just curious."

As Russell walked away, Nora stated, "We'll

skip arithmetic and literature for today since you are still getting used to this schoolwork, and all that business of the earthquake threw our schedule off a tad. How does it sound to deliver the rolls before lunch, and then you can have the afternoon to do whatever you'd like?"

"That sounds great," Evelyn agreed. "I just have a couple of flower names left to write." Once she finished, the two returned through the woods and stopped by the cottage for a little while. Nora put one last batch of bread in the oven while Evelyn checked on Pam to make sure the pigeon had enough water. There was still a pile of seeds in the crate, but the pigeon was hopping around inquisitively, pecking at the cracks between the floorboards.

Evelyn noticed that she had left her window propped open, so she shut it firmly. She didn't think Pam would be strong enough yet to fly up to the window, but just in case, she didn't want the bird to go wandering off before her wing was fully healed.

Not long after, the bread finished baking and the loaves were laid out on the counter, steaming and filling the house with a delicious aroma. Evelyn entered the kitchen to find Nora waiting at the front door, a couple of books tucked under one arm and the neatly packed basket of rolls on the other.

"You must let me carry the delivery. I always do," Evelyn insisted.

"It's not too heavy for me." Nora laughed. "I'll be fine."

"No, I insist," Evelyn persuaded. With a smile, Nora relinquished the load. The two stepped outside, and Nora shut the door to the cottage behind them. She locked it, and the two started for the village.

From where she stood on the path through the woods, Evelyn thought she saw a flicker of red and blue out of the corner of her eye in the trees by the cottage.

"Wait, Aunt Nora," she whispered. "Did you see that?"

Her aunt stopped and swiftly glanced from side to side. "What is it?" Nora asked, her voice matching the hush of Evelyn's.

"I thought I saw some movement in those trees over there," she said, pointing.

They waited, still and silent, and watched for a minute. Then Evelyn shook her head. "It's gone," she murmured. "Maybe I was imagining it."

"It could have been a woodland creature, or perhaps something falling from a tree," Nora suggested. "Shall we continue on?"

"Yes," said Evelyn, but she glanced back over her shoulder once more for good measure.

CHAPTER 7

"Now it's time for our first history lesson," Nora announced as she and Evelyn walked through Bluebell Forest. "We will begin with the ancient history of Heartsong."

Evelyn tilted her head to the side curiously. "I thought you said that a lot of our kingdom's history is unknown."

"That's right," Nora replied. "Much of it is legend, so no one knows for sure if it is true or not. And we don't have written records going back more than a hundred years, even though the kingdom is over four hundred years old."

"Why is that?" asked Evelyn. "Did the people not write very much?"

"People could definitely write—the places the kingdom traded with have documents dating back much further than four hundred years—but somehow Heartsong has nothing left from back then. Most of the information we have about those times was passed down orally, which can sometimes be an unreliable method, but we can be more certain it is true if we have artifacts or many similar stories to corroborate the legends. Personally, I believe there must have been records made and that something happened to them."

Nora shook her braid of gray hair over one shoulder. "Still, there are a few things we do know about the times before records were kept," she continued. "In the first place, there has always been a king or queen of Heartsong and Heartwood, and the two lands have always been friendly with each other. In the past, they rarely had trouble getting along, and when they did, the problem was always resolved."

Hopefully that will be the case now, thought Evelyn, remembering how her parents had decided to go to Heartwood before they could be prevented by the current disputes.

"A combined army, one of the best anyone knows of, defends both kingdoms. And, of course, there is also the huge Festival of Arts that is traditionally held every year, although it has been nearly ten years since the last one because of all the tensions and other disruptions in recent years. During the festival, the kingdoms come together to celebrate their unity, and Heartsong and Heartwood switch off hosting the event each time."

"I've heard of people from the village going, many years ago," Evelyn said. "One of our family's friends went, and she brought her finely woven cloth. She came back with some painted wooden birds that looked so lifelike it seemed they would take flight at any moment! She said the kings and queens give speeches, and then there is a huge show with all sorts of art: paintings and sculptures and wood carvings. There are stalls with food, and people sell their wares and crafts, too."

"That's right," agreed Nora. "It isn't hard to understand how Heartwood Kingdom got its name. There are many trees there that make for fine carving, and while, similarly to our kingdom, little of their ancient history is known, Heartwood seems to have always been renowned for its woodworking. There are many skilled carvers who export their works to other kingdoms far and wide, even places beyond the seas."

I'm glad that Heartwood doesn't have all *the beautiful trees*, Evelyn thought, walking through the wildflower-sprinkled forest. The creatures that had retreated to the shelter of their homes in the trees during the earthquake had come out once again, including a chipmunk that was scurrying around a fallen log.

Evelyn was intrigued by the history lesson and had already learned several things. *I almost wish I'd had more history lessons before*, she thought, warming to this part of Nora's plan for her education, at least. "Are any of the ancient carvings still left?" she asked.

"Yes, many are. In fact, there are carvings on display in glass boxes at our sister kingdom's castle that some people believe were made by one of the first kings of Heartwood. According to legend, that king loved woodworking and inspired many people to try to master it."

Nora paused momentarily while she and Evelyn carefully climbed over slick roots in a muddy area. On one side of the path was a wide pond with dozens of water lilies, their gently pointed petals curved to cradle orange-and-yellow centers. Floating on their round green leaves, the flowers made Evelyn think of teacups on delicate saucers. Giant willows thrived in the marshy soil, too, and trailed their leafy branches in the peaceful water.

Once past the soggy part of the path, Evelyn asked, "If Heartwood Kingdom got its name from the trees, how did Heartsong get its name?"

"Strangely enough, no one knows. It doesn't seem to be from any singing," Nora said. "Clearly, music doesn't seem to be a priority here, and it really never has been. Though some kingdoms are known for their instruments, very few people in Heartsong play any kind of music or even sing a lot."

"There's one person who plays instruments!" Evelyn chimed in.

"Who?" asked Nora, greatly interested.

"His name is Mr. Frost. People say he plays an instrument called an . . . organ, I believe it's called, but I've never seen one."

"I have a picture of one in a book. I will show you at home," Nora told her. "Have you heard the music of the organ?"

Evelyn shook her head. "Mr. Frost supposedly plays the accordion and banjo, too, and I've heard from people in the village that he used to come into town and play music every weekend. Since instruments are so rare in the kingdom, everyone loved and appreciated his playing, but that was before I was born."

"Why did he stop?" Nora asked. "What happened?"

"After his wife died, he became a recluse and never played again. He comes to the village very rarely for supplies, and he lives somewhere in the far reaches of Bluebell Forest."

The history lesson was so interesting that the time passed quickly, and soon Evelyn and Nora had left the shade of the narrow path through the woods, shifting to the cobblestone-paved street of the village. As they were walking, a man stepped out of the inn on the other side of the street and waved to them, a large newspaper in his hand flapping like the wing of a duck taking flight. "Good morning!" he called.

As Nora waved back politely, Evelyn said, "Nora, I'd like to introduce you to Mr. Whipple, the innkeeper. Mr. Whipple, this is my aunt, Nora."

"Ah, good to meet you," Nora greeted. "I suppose we've come to our destination."

Crossing the road with her aunt, Evelyn held up the basket. "Here are the rolls, baked fresh this morning as always!"

"Thank you," said Mr. Whipple with a friendly smile. "I appreciate you making the delivery even with all there must be to do now that your parents are gone."

"Of course," Evelyn replied, recalling that her parents had rented his wagon for their journey. She handed the basket of rolls to the innkeeper and was about to tell him that the millstone had broken, but the thought flitted across her mind that maybe she and Aunt Nora would find some solution soon. Then she remembered Oliver's peculiar interest in the mill and the millstone's markings, and she hesitated. By that time, though, the conversation had already moved on.

"Thankfully, we're making do so far," Nora said politely.

"I have some news you might be interested in, with your family traveling to Heartwood and all," Mr. Whipple informed them, passing his floppy newspaper to Evelyn. "You two can read this while you wait. I'll be back with the basket in a moment," he said, then turned to go into the inn.

Stepping closer to her aunt so Nora could read the article too, Evelyn unfolded the newspaper and held the large pages open with two hands. "Tensions Between Kingdoms Intensify," announced the headline. She felt her heart beat faster, wondering what the news could be and what it would mean for her family.

"According to reports from royal officials," Evelyn read aloud from the article, "Heart-song's king has declared that, for the tenth time in a row, his kingdom will not participate in the Festival of Arts this year. Since the kings' recent dispute about the army, the king of Heartwood has been threatening to close the border and cut off free trade between the kingdoms, a possibility that now seems all the more likely."

TENSIONS BETWEEN
KINGDOMS INTENSIFY

Oh no! thought Evelyn. *Will the border really close? Is my family going to get stuck in Heartwood?*

Soon Mr. Whipple came back outside to return the basket. He seemed ready to resume the conversation and discuss the contents of the newspaper, but seeing the troubled look on Evelyn's face, Nora excused them from the situation. "Thank you, Mr. Whipple, but we should get home now," she said. "Have a wonderful day."

Evelyn handed the newspaper back to the innkeeper and turned in the direction of home. At first she was mostly silent on the walk through the bustling streets and quiet woods, but then Nora spoke, trying to take her niece's mind off her worries.

"What are you going to do with the message you found on the pigeon?" Nora asked.

Evelyn smiled. She was growing to love Pam

and wished she could keep the bird rather than send it home. “Well, once the pigeon is better, I’ll release it with the original note. I am excited for the bird to heal so I can get the message to the person it was intended for. But I’m really curious, too, about what it means, especially because Bluebell Forest is my home, and no one I know has ever mentioned the legend the note refers to.”

“Are you going to add a message of your own?” questioned Nora.

“I’ve thought about writing something on the note or asking a question since I want to know if the legend has anything to do with the mill, but for some reason I don’t think I should. I’m going to watch Pam, though, to see which direction she flies when she’s well enough to be released. Maybe I can figure out where her home is, if it’s not too far away.”

By this time Evelyn and Nora were nearing

the cottage, and the silence in the air was deafening. There were no laughing voices of children to greet them, and there was no welcoming, familiar *splish*, *splish* of the mill wheel on the river. Evelyn's shoulders sagged as she remembered how much had changed in such a short time.

Noticing Evelyn's downtrodden demeanor, Nora brought up the mystery that had so entirely captured Evelyn's attention in an effort to distract her. "Isn't it an interesting coincidence that the first time any of us heard of Laughing Pipes Mill was right before the plaque with the same name got dug up?"

Evelyn shook herself a little and nodded, relieved to have something to focus on besides her worries. "I agree. I wonder who would have known about the plaque in the first place, and why they would dig it up now, of all times? It must have been called Laughing Pipes Mill in the time before we have written history, though I never would have believed it before seeing the inscription. Maybe somehow a record was preserved that mentions it, but even so, who would know about that? It seems unlikely that Oliver would have access to a rare ancient record."

"Perhaps the legend is from those long-ago days, too," Nora theorized.

"Do you think there really is a legend about the forest?" Evelyn asked.

Staring off into the distance, Nora was silent for a few steps and crossed her arms as she pondered. Seconds went by while she considered Evelyn's question.

"Maybe there really is." Nora pursed her lips. "So far, I don't have any ideas about who is looking into this legend or why, but the note the pigeon carried shows that something is clearly going on. Honestly, it makes me a little nervous that someone is sneaking around and we are unaware of why." Then she shook off her pensiveness and added, smiling, "But I do love a good mystery! I'm going to start asking the older people in the area if they know any legends about this forest. I've untangled more than a couple of knots in my history research that way."

They reached the yard and went into the cottage. *Something feels off*, Evelyn thought as she walked through the house. Everything in the kitchen was as tidy and clean as Nora had left it, and she could hear the chuckling sounds of the ferrets from Nora's room down the hallway.

When Evelyn opened the door to her own room, though, she knew what was wrong at once: Pam was gone. There was no happy coo when the door opened, and the pigeon was not in her crate or out exploring.

Where did she go? Evelyn wondered. She frantically began to search the room, and then she saw something that made her stop and stare. The window was halfway open. *I intentionally closed it before I left*, Evelyn remembered with shock.

"Aunt Nora, Aunt Nora!" she cried. "Pam is gone! Someone has taken her!"

CHAPTER 8

Mist was rising from the river the next morning as Evelyn stood near the mill, lovingly watering her family's rose garden. Dozens of bushes, thriving in the plot of rich soil, surrounded her. Some held only buds that promised to blossom soon, but others were in full bloom already and bore big open flowers in an array of colors: peach, dark pink, cheerful yellow, deep crimson, and every hue in between. Laden with so many roses, some branches drooped down to the soft, mossy earth.

In the quiet of the early hour, Evelyn pondered the previous day's events. She and Nora had searched all over the cottage, looking for any signs that someone had been in the house, but there were none. Nothing was out of place, and nothing had been stolen—aside from Pam, of course. Evelyn had been so concerned about someone possibly breaking into the house that she didn't want to sleep alone in her room, but Nora assured her that the cottage was locked up tight and sat with her until she fell asleep.

Wishing that she had been able to help Pam make a full recovery before the bird's disappearance, Evelyn also wondered why someone would have taken the carrier pigeon in the first place. She suddenly realized, *Now I won't be able to send the message back to where it was supposed to go. I may never find out what the legend means!* She felt a twinge of disappointment at the thought.

As Evelyn headed for the sandy riverbank to refill her watering can, her mind turned to her family and their journey, and she began to pray silently. *Father in Heaven, when will I hear from them?* she prayed. *Have they arrived at the doctor yet, and does he know how to help Mama? You know what she needs, so please give the doctor wisdom about what ails her.* She closed her eyes, thinking how delighted she would be if her family were able to return home sooner than expected. *Please let the cure work quickly.* Smiling with hope, Evelyn bent down and dipped her watering can in the gently flowing river, filling it to the brim. She returned to the garden to water the last few bushes, the ones with light pink roses.

Since tending to the rose garden was her favorite morning task, Evelyn had saved it for last, and now she was hungry. But before heading inside, she stopped at the mill to scoop up a handful of the leftover loose grain scattered over its floor. Nearing the cottage, she tossed it on the ground for the lively birds who frequented the yard in front of the bakery.

Inside the house, Nora was waiting with breakfast all ready, the room filled with tantalizing aromas. "I made a big meal because we have some important things to do today!" she said cheerily.

"Yes," Evelyn replied before her aunt could say anything about schoolwork. "We need to figure out what to do now that the mill's not working."

"Well, I wrote a letter to send to the doctor in Heartwood. He can give it to your family when they arrive. I didn't mention anything about the broken millstone yet, though; I don't want them to return before your mother is well. If we start running low on resources and have to close the bakery temporarily, I'm sure we can find something else to sell."

"Hmm. I'll start thinking about it and write down any ideas I have," Evelyn said. "Are you going to mail the letter when we go to the village today?"

"Yes, and I expect we might get a letter soon, too. Your mother said the family would send one as soon as they arrived in Heartwood. It is only a two-day journey, but it will probably take two or three more days for a letter to get to us."

After the two finished eating, Nora gathered up all the dishes in one perfectly balanced stack, then produced another list. Evelyn groaned. "Here is your schedule," Nora announced. "We'll start with handwriting again today."

Evelyn got her slate and chalk. "Are we going to go outside again?" she asked.

"No," said Nora, "I need to be here to do some baking. Look out the window, though, and watch the birds while I take this book I was reading earlier to my room."

Pushing a window open, Evelyn could hear the chirps, calls, and songs of birds, and she took a few moments to locate the sources of the different calls. Birds in different shades of gray were pecking at the grain Evelyn had scattered in the yard earlier, and she caught glimpses of birds with yellow and bits of blue in the trees. A wren flew over the yard, singing merrily.

When Nora came back, she pointed out, "Do you see how gracefully those birds are flying? It seems so smooth and effortless." Evelyn nodded. "I want you to write the names of the birds you see outside. Try to make your handwriting as graceful as they are."

"I can do that!" Evelyn replied. But as she looked down at her slate, out of the corner of her eye, she caught a glimpse of something brown and furry a few paces behind Nora. Freddy, the ferret, was trying to mimic Nora's steps, wobbling along on his hind feet. Evelyn giggled. The ferret stumbled, but he pushed himself back up and took three more steps.

"Aunt Nora, look behind you," Evelyn told her aunt mirthfully. Nora turned, not quite sure what to expect. When she saw her pet ferret staggering about, she chuckled.

"Come here, Freddy," Nora ordered in mock sternness. The ferret speedily ran over to her on all four paws and climbed up her dress, perching finally on her sleeve. With Freddy on her arm, Nora shuttled the ferret back to her room, shutting the door with a firm thud this time.

Evelyn returned her attention to her handwriting, filling the slate with names of the birds she loved. *Mourning dove, wren, chickadee . . .* she wrote. There weren't any pigeons in the yard this morning. *Sparrow, goldfinch, oriole . . .*

She soon finished. When Nora came to check Evelyn's work, she gave the girl a smile of approval. "Good work! With just a couple of days of focus, your handwriting is definitely getting more graceful."

Grinning, Evelyn said, "That was short and fun. What are we going to do now?"

"Let's do some arithmetic while we make the bread."

Evelyn felt a little skeptical about anything involving numbers, but she was willing to give it a try after how much she had enjoyed her other lessons so far. "Okay," she said. "What first?"

"While we shape these loaves of bread, we can go over multiplication. Do you know what that is?"

Her hands curved around a large velvety-smooth lump of dough, Evelyn paused to think. "That's when we add multiple groups of the same number, right?"

"Yes. Let's see, we're going to make three

diagonal slashes on each loaf of bread. How many slashes in total will there be on these eight loaves of bread? Try counting by threes."

"Hmm. Is it twenty-four?"

"Yes!" affirmed Nora. "Let's do some more practice."

Nora quizzed Evelyn aloud a few more times, and then they started mixing up another batch of dough. "This recipe is for a dozen rolls. Each batch needs three cups of flour, and we're going to make five batches. How many cups of flour will that take?"

Evelyn counted in her head. "That would be fifteen cups, I think," she said at last.

"That's right. Since it would take a long time to add everything over and over, it's very important to memorize your multiplication tables," Nora explained. "Doing so will take lots of practice, but we can make it fun. Let's have a contest."

"But I'm sure you will be so much faster than me," Evelyn pointed out.

"What if I form as many rolls as I can while you recite all the threes and fours times tables? I bet I can roll a dozen before you're done!"

"I can do it faster than that!" Evelyn exclaimed.

"Are you ready?" Nora prompted, sprinkling the counter with flour in preparation. "On your mark . . . get set . . . go!"

"Three times one is three, three times two is six . . ." Evelyn began.

The race was on. While Nora deftly shaped lumps of dough into smooth, pale rolls that looked like miniature snowballs, Evelyn flew through the threes as fast as she could. She was excited when she realized how well she was doing.

And then she got stuck. "Three times nine is . . ." Evelyn looked over at Nora. *No! She already has five rolls shaped!* She stopped to think. "Twenty-seven! And three times ten is thirty . . ." Evelyn hurried through the rest of the threes, then raced on through the fours, going as rapidly as she could.

Evelyn could see the rolls piling up, but she concentrated. "Four times eleven, forty-four, four times twelve, forty-eight. Finished!" called Evelyn.

"My, my! I only made ten rolls," said Nora.

Triumphant, Evelyn beamed. "Then I won! I like that game. Can we do it again?"

But before they could do any more arithmetic, from the forest came a clatter of wheels on the bumpy road. Evelyn peered out the window. "Who could it be?" she wondered, surprised.

"I have no idea," admitted Nora, a little puzzled. "We're not expecting anyone."

"People always walk when they come to the mill from the village," Evelyn explained as she ran outdoors. As the wagon came closer, Evelyn noticed how creaky it sounded. Weather-beaten and streaked, the wood on the sides was very old, too.

It turned into the clover-covered yard, and Evelyn was surprised at the number of occupants. Though the wagon had very few items compared to the one Nora had come in, it appeared to contain a whole family. A tall man drove, hunched to fit on the wagon's seat, and a

woman wearing a shawl sat next to him. There were two children, too: a girl about Evelyn's age and a boy a little younger.

Eager to meet the newcomers, Evelyn waved, and the children waved back. "Hello! I'm Evelyn. What are your names?" Evelyn asked.

Though the whole family looked somewhat rumpled from travel, the girl was cheerful. She had light red hair cut in a bouncy bob, and she wore a blue dress with lots of buttons. "I like

to go by my nickname, Birdie," she said with a friendly grin.

That's quite an unusual name, Evelyn mused.

"And I go by Pip!" the brother exclaimed enthusiastically. Evelyn nodded to the energetic boy with a smile.

"I'm eleven, and Birdie is thirteen," Pip volunteered as he swung himself down from the wagon. A satchel in his hand thumped against the wagon wheel as he landed.

Nora exited from the front door, sizing up the wagon and its contents with an observing glance. "Welcome," Nora greeted the family. "How are you today? Can we assist you with something?"

"We're glad to have gotten here safely, thank you," the father said as he climbed down from the driver's seat, wincing as he stretched his long legs. He held out his hand to help his wife down from the wagon.

He continued, "We were actually wondering if you might be willing to help us, but not as bakery customers."

What could they possibly want? Evelyn wondered.

CHAPTER 9

Seeing the expectant, questioning looks on Evelyn's and Nora's faces, the tall man explained, "I have urgent business in Heartwood Kingdom, but we feel that it is unsafe for the whole family to travel there at present because of the disunity."

Evelyn felt a tug in her stomach as she pictured her parents and three siblings, who were hopefully in Heartwood at that very moment. She could certainly relate to this man's concerns. *I hope they're okay*, she thought.

“My children and I need a place to stay until my husband can return,” said the mother. She had a calm, soothing voice, but Evelyn was shocked at what she heard next. “We were wondering, could we pay to stay with you and eat here for a few weeks until his business is finished?”

Then the woman offered a handsome amount that made Evelyn stare with wide eyes. *That is a lot! It would get us through a few weeks of expenses*, Evelyn realized. *But why us?* Though this seemed like a strange situation, the parents were evidently quite serious.

She could tell Nora was thinking along the same lines. “That is a very generous offer. We’ll need to step inside for a moment to consider,” her aunt told the couple.

“Of course,” the father replied as Evelyn and Nora went into the cottage, closing the door partway.

"They seem very kind and are in need of a place to stay. I think it will be safe and that we should help them. What are you thinking?" asked Nora.

Evelyn smiled. Although she had loved this time getting to know her aunt, the house sometimes felt too quiet and empty without her family. Though Evelyn would still miss her siblings acutely, this seemed like the perfect chance to have some children around her own age at home. She admitted to Nora, "I'd really enjoy having Birdie and Pip here. They seem kind and interesting. I'd love to get to know more about them. And with just the two of us right now, we have the extra room. Would it make more work for you, though?"

Nora shook her head. "I don't mind, and we could use the extra money with the mill and bakery in the state they are."

Grinning, Evelyn said, "Let's go for it, then!"

Back outside, Nora announced their decision: "You're welcome to stay here." Relief appeared on the parents' faces, and Pip and Birdie looked very excited. "Can we help you bring your bags inside?" Nora offered.

"I must get going as soon as possible, so would it be fine if we just stacked them in the yard for the moment?" the father asked.

As Nora, Evelyn, Birdie, Pip, and the two parents worked together to unload the few pieces of luggage onto the thick clover, Evelyn contemplated the sudden visitors. Travelers were always coming through the forest, and at times, her family had hosted strangers for a day or two before they continued on their journey. But it seemed a little odd that people who were willing to pay that much would come in such a dilapidated, run-down wagon. Evelyn shrugged off the mysterious circumstances. *I'll just wait and see if I can get some answers while they're here.*

The unloading was soon finished, and the father hugged each member of his family before quickly hopping into the wagon. "Goodbye!" he called over his shoulder. For a while after he drove off, Evelyn could still hear the horse's hooves clopping at a brisk rate.

Then Evelyn realized that neither the father nor mother had introduced themselves. Nora must have been thinking the same thing, for at that precise moment, she turned to the mother and asked, "What is your name?"

The mom laughed a little nervously. "Since my son and daughter are going by their nicknames, I might as well, too. I'm Rosie because I love roses."

These nickname introductions are strange, Evelyn thought. Was it a family tradition? Were Rosie and her children hiding something, or did they simply value their privacy? *Whatever their reasoning, I really like them anyway.*

With a gracious smile, Nora offered, "Well, if you love roses, I have just the lunch for you. You must try some of my rose jam and rose hip tea."

As she gazed after the two women, who began chatting warmly while they headed into the cottage, Evelyn noticed Birdie and Pip watching, too. Evelyn gave them a smile. "I think they're going to be perfect friends for each other," she predicted.

"I agree!" Birdie laughed, and Evelyn thought it was the most pleasant, melodious laugh she'd ever heard.

"I'm so glad you've come to stay here. I can't wait to show you around and go exploring."

"Oh yes! I hope we have lots of adventures in Bluebell Forest," Birdie proclaimed excitedly.

Staggering under the weight of a plump carpetbag, Pip shouldered yet another bag, and Birdie dropped back to help. *He reminds me of my brother Jacob*, Evelyn thought. *They're almost the same age, too.* She felt a tightening in her chest and hurried forward to hold the door.

Just then, Pip dropped one of the bags he was carrying, and it burst open when it hit the ground. Birdie helped him gather the scattered items, quickly packing the bag and handing it back to Pip. He laughed and thanked her before whispering, "I can't believe we get to stay at Laughing Pipes Mill!"

Evelyn's heart nearly stopped. *How do they know that name?*

A movement in the sky caught Evelyn's eye. High above her, the dark silhouette of a falcon was circling. Oliver's falcon.

Questions flew into Evelyn's mind: *How did Birdie's family and Oliver know this mill used to be called Laughing Pipes Mill? Who uncovered the plaque and stole the pigeon from my room? Is there really a legend about this forest, and what is it?*

"Are you all right?" Birdie asked.

But Evelyn didn't hear. She was staring at the old stone mill and the forest that loomed above it, wondering what secrets they might hold.

CHAPTER 10

Evelyn was roused from sleep by the distant, haunting melody emanating from the hills. *There it is again! Where is that music coming from?* she wondered as she had hundreds of times before. She sprang out of bed quickly and opened her window to hear it better. *The music almost never comes in the morning*, she reflected. Sitting at the window seat, Evelyn felt the cool, damp morning mist seeping into her room while she listened to the faraway sound. *Perhaps it is the wind whistling through the mountains*, she speculated. *Could it be that it has always been there, even in the ancient days? Maybe the music is why the kingdom is called Heartsong.*

Hearing a gentle moo from the direction of the barn reminded Evelyn that the animals needed to be taken care of, so she rose from her drowsy position at the window seat and got ready for the day.

She went into the kitchen, where Nora was making bread, her apron already dusted with flour. No one else was up yet; in the two days they had stayed at the cottage, Birdie, Pip, and Rosie had yet to grow used to waking up as early as Evelyn and her aunt did to prepare all the bread.

"Good morning," Evelyn said. "I'm heading outside to do the chores in the farmyard. Do you mind if I go on a walk after I finish?"

"That's fine," Nora replied, then displayed her hands, which were covered with the sticky dough she was kneading, and asked, "Would you go to my room and get the schedules I've made for Pip and Birdie and also a pen to check off their lists? They'll need them when they wake up."

Evelyn nodded and went down the hall. Since Rosie was not used to teaching her children's lessons, Nora had volunteered to help them with their schoolwork. Some villages had schoolhouses, Evelyn knew, although she had never traveled far enough to see one, so she assumed Birdie and Pip had attended one of those. They enjoyed Nora's teaching and didn't seem to mind the schedules as much as Evelyn had at first.

She hesitated at the door of Nora's room. After her startling first encounter with Freddy, Evelyn had avoided the room full of ferrets. Though she usually adored animals, she was a little nervous around these peculiar-looking creatures. But Evelyn could hear no sound coming from behind the door. *Maybe they're sleeping*, she thought as she slowly opened the door and stepped inside quietly.

As it so happened, that was not the case. When the five ferrets noticed Evelyn's entrance, they began to dart around rapidly in excitement, not seeming to mind that they were bumping into walls and furniture. The floor was filled with creatures dashing in all directions, and Evelyn was afraid to move and risk stepping on one of their long tails. A medley of chirps and barks and a sound that was almost like a laugh filled the room as the furry ferrets bounded here and there.

Evelyn didn't know what to do. She wanted to step out into the hall, but then one of the frenzied creatures might escape. *What if these noisy ferrets wake up our guests?* she worried. *They're just on the other side of the hall, and I don't want them to be tired all day.* As she was trying to think of some way to get the animals to calm down, she remembered how much Pam, the pigeon, liked it when Evelyn stroked her. *Maybe it will work with the ferrets, too.*

Of all the ferrets, Freddy was whirring around the most energetically, but he was the first that happened to come within Evelyn's reach. He bumped into one of the legs of the bed, stumbled, then started running the other way . . . right toward Evelyn. She grabbed hold of him and tried to pet his fur in a soothing way, but he wriggled and wriggled and did not seem to be getting any calmer.

At last, Freddy slipped out of Evelyn's grasp and ran straight up her spine, finally perching on her head! Evelyn could feel the ferret's tiny paws tightly gripping her hair. *Oh no! What am I going to do?* she wondered in consternation.

Then Freddy sprang off, landing with a squeal on the bed, and burrowed into the pillows.

Evelyn breathed a sigh of relief. Without him leading the antics, the other ferrets settled down, and Evelyn could easily find what she needed.

She soon re-entered the kitchen with a quill pen, an inkwell, and a few sheets of paper. The whole adventure had lasted only a few minutes, but Nora had gotten quite a lot done, and two dozen smooth loaves of bread lay in an array on the counter. "I'll just set these on the table so they don't get dirty," Evelyn offered, holding up the papers.

"Thank you," said Nora with a reflective note in her voice. She looked around, checking to be sure none of the visitors were nearby. More quietly, she said, "I've been pondering why the mill was originally named Laughing Pipes Mill. I've had some ideas, but I haven't fully figured it out."

"You mean, what the word 'pipes' in the title

refers to?" Evelyn's curiosity was piqued.

"Yes. I don't think it means a pipe like people smoke. Perhaps it means there are pipes for water, but those wouldn't laugh, I think. It seems more likely that it would involve pipes like a musical instrument." Clearly, Nora had been thinking about this at length, trying to put pieces together in the same way she did her history research.

"Maybe an organ like Mr. Frost plays?" suggested Evelyn.

"Yes, or the three-holed flute that some people call a pipe. Though instruments are rare now, perhaps that was not the case when the mill was built. The name really baffles me so far," Nora admitted, "but I want to know the mill's history. Perhaps it is connected to the legend."

Evelyn thought about Nora's idea as she went around the yard collecting the eggs, milking the cows, and watering the roses. *If no one living at the mill knows what the pipes are, perhaps its name was changed to conceal that the pipes were here, whatever they are.* She still had not asked Birdie and Pip how they knew the mill's original name, and nothing else about their family had seemed unusual. *Maybe it's time to ask them what they know about Laughing Pipes Mill,* Evelyn thought. Would they refuse to answer? Their family did keep their background private, not even sharing their real names, but surely they would be willing to share with Evelyn anything they knew about her home.

When Nora mentioned the mystery of the mill, though, Evelyn also remembered something that she had almost completely forgotten: the faint alphabet etched on the now-cracked millstone. While she didn't really see their significance, Oliver had been so intrigued by the letters and symbols that Evelyn wondered if they had some purpose. After all, Oliver knew about the other name for the mill, so maybe he knew more about the building.

After she finished watering the rosebushes, where more buds had been bursting into blossoms every day for the past week, Evelyn began her walk, starting down the path that traipsed through the thickest growths of trees. Ferns lined her way, and the feathery fronds reached into her path, as if trying to tickle her as she brushed past them.

Evelyn couldn't imagine any place in the world being more beautiful or special than Bluebell Forest. This morning, the shadows the trees cast in the radiant morning light dappled the forest floor with strokes of sun and shade, making the thick carpet of bluebells appear to hold every tint from lavender and brilliant amethyst to a deep midnight purple. A few buttercups and tiny white flowers had raised their heads among the bluebells, too, and patches of wildflowers delicately swayed as a gentle breeze touched them.

A few more minutes of walking brought Evelyn to one of her favorite climbing trees. Ivy clung to its thick bark, and its large, low branches were perfect footholds for scaling the high boughs, where Evelyn loved to sit. From there she could see far, even to the pond with the pink water lilies and graceful willows. She realized that with her new school schedule and helping out in the bakery, she hadn't been up in a tree since the day her family left for Heartwood.

Evelyn was about to begin her ascent when she saw something in the sky. *Could it be?* Flying over the treetops was a pigeon, and though she had often seen them in the forest, this one had a flash of green that appeared now and then as it angled its wings to catch the wind. Closer and closer the pigeon flew, and Evelyn could soon make out a patch of shiny green feathers on its neck—just like Pam's. And even more surprising, there seemed to be something white on its orange leg. *Could this bird be bearing a message? Is it another carrier pigeon, or is it Pam?*

Hoping to discover what direction the bird was going, Evelyn ran through the forest, glancing up frequently to try to keep sight of the pigeon while weaving between the towering trees. But at last, panting, she gave up. The pigeon was much too swift to follow.

Slowly, she walked back to the house. The many mysteries flying around the forest and the bakery were much like the pigeon—escaping out of her reach. Though Evelyn wanted to know where the pigeon was headed, she was equally curious about where it had come from. The original message on Pam's leg had said that the sender—and somebody else—was safe here in Bluebell Forest. Could Oliver have sent Pam? He had just arrived, although no one else had been with him the two times he and Evelyn had seen each other. He had been really eager about Pam at first, but anyone who was interested in animals would have wanted to help the hurt pigeon. And besides, he had said the pigeon wasn't his. Oliver wouldn't have lied, would he?

She shook her head. *I want to trust Oliver, and I think he was telling the truth. But I think he knows something about the forest that he isn't sharing, too.*

CHAPTER 11

When Evelyn entered the warm, yeasty-smelling kitchen, Rosie was watching pancakes cook into puffy golden rounds, a spatula in her hand, while Nora was pouring ingredients into a saucepan for buttermilk syrup. "Are these ready to flip yet?" Rosie asked.

"Here, come stir this while I check," Nora replied pleasantly.

"I hope this syrup doesn't burn," Rosie said, unsure of herself, rapidly mixing the pan's contents with all her might.

"It will be fine, even if you don't stir it so hard," Nora assured her patiently.

Otherwise elegant and collected, Rosie was anything but confident in the kitchen. In the two days since the family had arrived, Rosie and Nora had started becoming friends, and the two were always working together. Rosie loved helping Nora, but she seemed to not know how to do the most basic cooking and cleaning. Nora never got frustrated with her, though, and was willing to patiently teach her without appearing to notice how little Rosie could do.

While Nora finished making breakfast, Rosie set the table and arranged the food in beautiful patterns, but then she tried to cut up some strawberries with a huge butcher knife. It did not work very well.

When she attempted to wipe the counter clean a few minutes later, she left huge streaks of water everywhere and didn't wring out the rag when she was done. Then she poured some pancake batter into the skillet but forgot to add butter first, and the whole batch stuck to the pan.

At last, Nora asked, "Rosie, are you feeling all right? Do you need a break? I can see that you seem a little stressed right now."

Rosie sighed. "It's just that I'm no good at helping around the house. I enjoy doing it, but I feel like I'm making things harder for you." Then, after a long pause, she admitted, "To be honest, I've always had servants to help me at my home."

Evelyn was surprised by that information, and she could tell that Nora was, too, by the way her eyebrows shot up.

However, Nora tried to act nonchalant. "Well, don't worry about that. You don't need to learn everything at once. It's normal to make mistakes while you're gaining experience. You will feel much better after you eat something."

Once breakfast was ready, everyone sat down at the table, and Nora gave a prayer of thanks for the food. Evelyn was hungry but also excited to tell about the pigeon she had seen now that everyone was gathered around.

"Guess what I saw today in the forest!" she began eagerly. Rosie's family and Nora all turned their eyes to Evelyn. "I saw a pigeon flying over the treetops this morning, and I'm almost certain it had a message attached to its leg!"

"A carrier pigeon?" Pip asked in delight.

"Yes, I think so!" Evelyn replied. "I've seen one only once before, but the one I saw today had the same sort of feathers on its neck that were on that other pigeon."

"When was the first time?" Rosie inquired, intrigued.

"I was walking in the forest less than a week ago when I saw an injured pigeon that was attacked by a falcon. When I went to help it, I found a message tied to its leg."

Rosie frowned a little. "There was a falcon? I thought no one could hunt here since most of Bluebell Forest belongs to the royal family and the kingdom."

Evelyn remembered that Mama had said something similar. She shrugged. "Well, the boy the falcon returned to said he was just exercising it. It was clear he didn't intend for the falcon to bring down the pigeon."

Birdie leaned in excitedly and pushed a loose strand of light red hair behind her ear. "Please, tell us what you did with the pigeon!"

"Well, first of all, I named her Pam," Evelyn continued. "Then I brought her home and kept her in my room so I could help her heal and get well. But a few days ago, she just mysteriously went missing."

"Did she fly away?" asked Pip.

Evelyn shook her head. "She was stolen. The window to my bedroom was open, and I had definitely shut it."

Birdie, Pip, and their mother looked at each other, wide-eyed. "That is quite surprising. I'm sure I haven't heard of many people who use carrier pigeons," Rosie said. While the discussion soon turned to other things, Evelyn was left wondering about the pigeon—and where Pam had come from.

Later, after the meal was cleaned up, Nora gave a history lesson to the children while they sat at the kitchen table with their chalk and slates. She had suggested that they draw something interesting from the discussion of the kingdom's history. After Nora's encouragement that morning, Rosie had decided to sit in on the school sessions and was seated in a comfortable chair in the corner.

For the benefit of the new students, Nora

asked, "Evelyn, do you remember what Heartwood is known for?"

"It has a lot of good trees that the people use for woodworking and making amazing carvings," Evelyn answered. Birdie and Pip nodded in agreement.

"That's right. With all the beautiful things they create, their kingdom brings in a lot of money. No one else in the world has mastered woodworking like they have," Nora explained. She opened a book that was next to her and searched for a picture. "Ah, here it is. This is a drawing of some of the carvings rumored to be made by one of Heartwood's early kings." She showed the image to everyone sitting around the table, and Evelyn looked at it appreciatively.

When Evelyn had first seen all the books Nora had brought with her, she wondered why her aunt needed so many, but she soon realized how impressive and useful Nora's collection was. Besides the stories Evelyn had started to read, her aunt also had scores of nonfiction books, many of which had pictures.

Nora turned to another page and continued with her lesson. "Since their beginnings, the sister kingdoms have always had a shared army, and they split its costs equally between themselves. But the king of Heartsong does not believe that is fair anymore."

"Why not?" asked Evelyn. "Hasn't it worked for hundreds of years?"

"Heartwood has accumulated greater riches than Heartsong, and the people make so much more money there," Nora explained. "Since a recent census showed that there are now many more people in Heartwood, too, that means individuals in Heartsong are taxed more for the army."

"I can see why that seems unfair. But why is the king of Heartsong so angry? He could just say no," Evelyn pointed out.

"Well, once this issue came up, Heartsong's king said some things against the character of the king of Heartwood, and they began to argue. Now they both dislike each other, and there have been a lot of tensions festering since then, but no open conflict. Nothing has actually happened yet, but the root of these problems has not been solved."

"I remember seeing things about that in the newspapers," Evelyn said. "So all these tensions come from the dispute over whether or not Heartwood should have to pay more for the army?"

"That's right," confirmed Nora.

As the lesson continued, Evelyn realized that Birdie and Pip weren't making the usual energetic comments that had punctuated the history discussions since they arrived. When she looked over at the two siblings, both had their heads bent low and were intently working on their drawings of castles. Though she could not see their expressions, it seemed to Evelyn that they were in a serious mood.

Why are Pip and Birdie being so unusually quiet? Evelyn wondered.

CHAPTER 12

When Evelyn stepped outside, she closed her eyes to the intense brilliance of the midmorning sunshine that dazzled her vision. Today, she and Nora had a few errands to do in town besides delivering rolls. They both were so eager to check the post office for a letter from Evelyn's family that they decided to go to the village before doing schoolwork. Also, having turned away a handful of visitors to the mill in the past three days, they decided to post an announcement in the village that Misty Creek Mill would be out of order until further notice.

Looking around while she waited for her aunt, Evelyn spotted Birdie sitting in the shade of a tree, braiding bluebells into a crown. "Would you like to join us this morning?" Evelyn asked. "I don't believe you've gotten a chance to see the village yet."

Birdie shook her head. "I'd rather stay home today." Since the history lesson the day before, she had been a bit pensive, and Evelyn wondered if Birdie was worried about something. She had not asked her friend about it, though, and hoped Birdie would soon feel like her normal perky self.

"All right, then. Enjoy the morning and the beautiful weather."

The front door opened, and Nora came out with the long-used basket heaped with rolls. Today, she had also included a small jar of rose jam. "The innkeeper might enjoy it. I wanted to give him a gift," she explained. "He is always

so friendly and willing to share the latest news with us."

Smiling, Evelyn said, "Mr. Whipple has always been a wonderful, helpful neighbor." Her aunt, so kind and thoughtful, was always pointing out the good in people they met and cheering others on. Just today she had pointed out Rosie's persistence as she learned about housecleaning and complimented her on how pristine the floor was once she swept it after breakfast. For Evelyn, sweeping would have been an easy task, but Nora understood what each person needed and recognized how difficult it was for Rosie to wield a broom the first few times.

As Evelyn and her aunt walked through the forest, Evelyn noticed ferns and a few red wildflowers that had appeared only in the past couple of days, their growth probably hastened by the light afternoon showers that were common during summer. The season was unfolding quickly, and already the leaves on the trees were turning a richer green.

Flowing near the path, the river murmured as it met a cluster of rocks in its path and washed a fallen branch downstream. A mother duck and her six ducklings swam near the bank. "Aunt Nora," Evelyn asked with sudden curiosity, "the river leads to the sea, but where does it come from?"

"Melting snow from the mountains feeds the river, and it passes the royal palace and takes a long, winding path through the countryside before it reaches us," she answered.

A piercing screech abruptly resounded through the forest, interrupting any further discussion. Startled, Evelyn scanned the sky. There was the falcon swooping over the treetops. She had grown used to these irregular interruptions by the bird. *Is Oliver nearby?* she wondered.

Glancing around, she saw a figure up the hill disappear into the bushes. Evelyn couldn't quite tell, but she thought she had seen the swirl of a skirt and maybe a girl's plaited hair. She studied the bushes and then shook her head. *Perhaps I was wrong*, she thought, spotting Oliver tramping among the trees near the cluster of bushes, carrying a dead rabbit over his shoulder. Evelyn would have liked to talk with him again, but he was out of hearing range and briskly passed through the thicket of bushes. Once again, she pondered what Oliver was doing in the forest and where he was staying. Hopefully he had caught the rabbit on private property, otherwise he'd get in trouble for illegally hunting in Bluebell Forest. Evelyn wondered if someone *had* gone through the bushes before Oliver did. Neither time Evelyn had spoken with Oliver had he mentioned someone being with him.

"There he is again. What can he be doing here? He ought to come and visit us sometime," Nora remarked, following Evelyn's gaze. "I would make him some of those delicious muffins he missed out on after the earthquake!" She and Evelyn had halted at the commotion of the falcon, but now they continued their moderate pace.

"I wonder about Oliver, too," Evelyn replied. "Have you ever looked in your books to see if Elk Grove, where he came from, is on any maps?"

Nora tilted her head. "No, I suppose I haven't. If I remember, I'll try to find it this afternoon." Of the many crates of books Nora had brought, one was entirely filled with maps and books on various kingdoms and their geography. Evelyn's aunt had used them to show her the route her family would likely take to Heartwood.

Now more than ever, Evelyn yearned for a letter from her family. *Why is it taking so long for the letter to arrive? They should be in Heartwood by now.* Having reached the cobblestone road to the village, Evelyn felt her heart beat a little faster with anticipation. How she wished for a letter, and oh, how she longed for her family!

The post office was a small building beside the inn, where both stagecoaches and mail wagons were constantly arriving and stopping to deliver goods or let their passengers get a meal. Unlike the stone cottage where Evelyn's family dwelled, most of the village buildings were made of wood but were nevertheless sturdy and had stood where they were for ages.

As Evelyn and Nora stepped through the doorway of the post office, a bell rang above their heads. At first the room appeared empty, but then the postmaster stood up from his desk in the back of the room and peeked his head over the small square cubbies that held the sorted mail. "Hello!" he greeted them. "What can I do for you today?"

"We're hoping for a letter from Evelyn's family," Nora replied. "Has one arrived yet, by chance?"

The postmaster shook his head. "No, not yet," he replied sympathetically. "I haven't gotten anything addressed to you in the past few days."

Evelyn tried not to let her countenance fall. "Well, we have a letter to send while we're here anyway." She produced an envelope from the pocket of her dress, which contained one sheet each from Nora and Evelyn. Evelyn's much-improved handwriting graced the front of the envelope, directing it to the care of the doctor in Heartwood for delivery to her family.

The postmaster took it. "I will do my best to get it there safely. Things are very uncertain at the borders between the kingdoms right now."

Nora thanked the postmaster, and Evelyn seconded the thanks with a neighborly smile. On their way out, Evelyn asked, "Should we go to the inn now? Then our basket will be empty when we do our shopping."

"No," Nora responded thoughtfully, "I think that we should go to Mr. Lampton's shop first today." She shrugged. "I don't know why. But we only have a few small purchases to make, so they will be easy to carry until we deliver the rolls."

"All right," Evelyn agreed. Only a few houses stood between the post office and shop, and they soon arrived. Evelyn opened the weighty wooden door, knowing from experience that it required a hard push to budge. Inside, Mr. Lampton was balanced on a ladder, trying to hoist a barrel lying on its side down from a shelf.

"Hello, and stand clear!" the shopkeeper greeted as he saw his customers enter.

For how small the village was, Mr. Lampton kept his shop stocked with quite an assortment of goods brought from many kingdoms. On the shelves were bottles of olive oil, gleaming brass pots, boxes with an aroma that hinted of chocolate, tiny glass beads, straw brooms made by hand, flower seeds, baskets, colorful thread, chalk, ginger root, buttons, and dozens of other things. Large barrels of salt and sugar were arranged on the floor, and more were up out of the way, waiting to be lifted down. Sacks of oats and dried corn that farmers brought to barter for their purchases were piled in a corner, too.

"Good morning," Evelyn said, watching as the shopkeeper carefully eased the barrel into his arms and descended the ladder.

"Is there anything I can assist you two with today?" Mr. Lampton asked.

"We just need a few ingredients and a spool of twine, if you have one," Nora replied. Pip had been mentioning he wanted to make a kite, but Evelyn and her aunt hadn't found anything in the house that was both long and sturdy enough for the string. "Also, the mill was damaged by the earthquake, and we were wondering if you would let us post a notice outside your store that it is closed."

"Of course," nodded the shopkeeper. "As there's not a farmer or villager who doesn't stop by here often, I'm sure my patrons would appreciate the information."

Through the wide window at the front of the store, Evelyn could see someone walking on the other side of the street whom she, surprisingly, did not know: an elderly man with a shock of white hair, who was bent under a large, lumpy knapsack tossed over his shoulders. His clothes and boots were old and worn, spattered in mud from what appeared to have been a long journey. His expression was stern, his eyebrows knitted together, and his lips permanently drawn into a tight pucker. *Another newcomer?* she wondered. Between Rosie's family and Oliver, more people had been coming to the area than usual. Then an inkling of remembrance crossed her mind. Something about the man was familiar. Where had she seen him before?

It's Mr. Frost! Evelyn realized. He had come to the mill to buy flour from Papa on a few occasions over the years, not appearing to mind the long walk through Bluebell Forest despite his evident age. Mr. Frost was not known for being a social person and was rarely seen. In fact, Evelyn had never actually spoken to him.

"Ah, Mr. Frost!" Mr. Lampton greeted cheerfully as Mr. Frost pushed through the heavy door of the store. "In town for your usual supplies? It's been months since I've last seen you in the village!"

In response, Mr. Frost gave only a small grunt and began moving silently about the shop.

It makes sense that he only needs to make the journey to buy supplies once in a while, she thought, *but the main reason he keeps to himself must be that he doesn't want to come down. He seems so grumpy, as if he detests being around people*. Stealing another glance, Evelyn could see that the elderly man wore a stern expression.

At that moment, two small children came running around a corner hand in hand, and they both collided with Mr. Frost. Evelyn recognized them as the six-year-old twins whose parents ran the local weaving business. The little girl picked herself up with ease and dusted off her elbows, but her twin brother's mouth was quivering, and he looked as though he were about to cry.

Mr. Frost's face smoothed into an expression that was not quite so stern, and he leaned down to help the boy. The little girl seemed to be explaining something as she pointed at the ground, and Evelyn noticed a limp little drawstring bag in the brother's hand. Then Mr. Frost started picking up things off the floor. What was he doing?

Marbles, Evelyn realized. She knew how the twins loved to show people their colorful glass marbles and think of new uses for them, and small as it seemed, she understood the young boy's disappointment.

Now grumpy Mr. Frost was taking the time to chase after the marbles that had scattered everywhere when the children ran into him. *That is so kind!* Evelyn thought. *Surely he must be more friendly than people make him out to be.*

By the time Mr. Frost finished, though, he had resumed his gruff demeanor and continued moving silently about the shop collecting various goods.

As she and Nora gathered the items they needed, Evelyn puzzled over Mr. Frost's kindness to the small children and its contrast with how he normally appeared. Suddenly, Evelyn wondered, *Is he lonely? After all, few people talk to him now that he only rarely comes to the village. Is there any way I can help him feel more welcome?* She shook her head. Maybe he would rather not interact with anyone. Or maybe she just needed to have a little courage. Admittedly, talking to Mr. Frost did not seem very pleasant, but she reminded herself, *I am one of his nearest neighbors since he lives in Bluebell Forest, too. It surely wouldn't offend him if I said hello at least.*

Then Evelyn had an idea. "Mr. Lampton, may I use some of your wrapping paper?" she asked.

"Sure," the shopkeeper replied, looking a little surprised at the request.

Quietly, Evelyn explained to Nora, "I think

Mr. Frost is lonely, and I'd like to give him a gift to let him know that we're thinking of him. Do you think it would be all right to give him some of the rolls we brought?"

Smiling, Nora whispered, "I think that's an excellent idea. Who wouldn't like some freshly baked rolls, especially ones from our bakery?" Then she drew the jar of rose jam out of the basket. With sunlight from the window shining through its rich, translucent red, it looked like a bright ruby. "Here, put this with the rolls, too. I can bring some jam for the innkeeper another day."

"Thank you," Evelyn said, taking the jar. Nora followed her to the large spool of coarse brown paper that rested near the shop's counter, and they picked a half dozen light, fluffy rolls to wrap into a neat parcel with the jam. After she cut a generous length of twine, Evelyn tied the string into a loopy, elaborate bow on top.

By this time, Mr. Frost had found what he needed, paid his bill, and was standing in a corner trying to arrange all his purchases snugly into his knapsack. Cradling her bundle in both hands, Evelyn walked over and stood beside him.

What should I say? she wondered. Mr. Frost turned his gaze to Evelyn. She cleared her throat. "Hello. I don't believe we've met, but I'm Evelyn from Misty Creek Mill. You're Mr. Frost, aren't you?"

"Yes," he said curtly.

Rushing on, Evelyn continued, "Since we so rarely get to see you, I wanted to give you a little gift from our bakery. I hope you enjoy it." She held the present out.

With both white eyebrows raised, Mr. Frost looked scrutinizingly at her. And then, to Evelyn's surprise, Mr. Frost smiled. It was just a little smile, but the lines at the corners of his eyes crinkled in pleasure.

"Thank you," he said gently and dipped his head. Then he paused a moment before lifting his knapsack and turning to go on his way.

As Evelyn watched him cross the street, she heard Nora softly remark, "What a puzzling old man."

CHAPTER 13

Nora had announced that she was in a jam-making mood, so Birdie, Pip, and Evelyn decided to gather some of the blackberries that grew near the river. They enjoyed eating the delicious fruit as they filled their baskets.

Pip had been picking the most ardently of the three, and it seemed that the brambles had retaliated. From the elbow down, his arms were covered in scratches from the tiny thorns on the blackberry bushes, and he had streaks of berry juice on one cheek, on both sleeves, and somehow on his socks, too.

As she picked methodically, Birdie caught a glimpse of her brother's arms. "Why don't you run some cool river water over your scratches? It might make them feel better," she suggested.

Shaking his head, Pip said determinedly, "I'm going to pick the most. See, my basket is the fullest! You'll get ahead of me if I stop."

"We could all take a break," Evelyn offered, a hint of an amused smile on her lips. "Then we would be even."

"Okay!" agreed Pip enthusiastically. "That would be perfect." Thumping his basket down on the ground, he dashed to the riverbank.

Evelyn set her basket at the base of a tree and wiped the perspiration from her face with the back of her hand. The weather had been pleasantly warm in the morning but had gotten more and more humid as the day went on. Hopefully Mr. Frost hadn't gotten too exhausted on his hike back to his secluded home in the hills.

"Let's wait up in one of these trees and surprise Pip when he gets back," Birdie proposed mischievously. "Remember when we were playing hide-and-seek yesterday? It was ten minutes before we could find where he had hidden in that tree, even though he kept tossing acorns down at us wherever we went."

Chuckling at the recent memory, Evelyn followed as Birdie scaled a tree. Up in the branches, a cool breeze tried to coax Evelyn's long hair out of its braid and ruffled Birdie's light red hair, too. As Evelyn settled herself onto a limb of the tree, one leg tucked beneath her, she felt something small shift beneath her foot. She didn't move for a moment, not sure what was there. Then she felt for the object with her hand.

In the crevice where the branch met the trunk was a small, smooth, odd-shaped piece of wood that was certainly not part of the tree. "I think I've found something," Evelyn breathed.

Birdie moved closer. “What is it?”

Evelyn picked up the small object and examined it. “It looks like a wood carving, but it’s unfinished.”

She handed it to Birdie, who turned it over and over and ran her fingers across the intricate details. “It’s carved in the style that is used in Heartwood,” Birdie commented.

Evelyn furrowed her brow, puzzled. “Why would this be here, then, up in a tree?”

Birdie shook her head, wondering. “Could there be a spy? Or maybe it’s from long ago.”

“No, it looks fresh and not at all weathered.” Evelyn shrugged. “I wonder what the carver was trying to make.” Holding it closer to eye level, Evelyn rotated the object in her hand. Half of it was partially polished and had the fine details that Heartwood woodwork was known for, while the other half had an indistinct form.

Then Evelyn drew in a sharp breath. “I know

what this is supposed to be! It's a carrier pigeon, just like the bird I was caring for. The head and one of the feet aren't finished yet, but this is a leg, I'm sure of it, with a cylinder attached that looks just like the message that was tied to Pam."

Her eyes widening, Birdie asked, "But who besides you would be familiar with how carrier pigeons look? They're so rare."

"And who was working on this while they were so near to the house and mill? There really aren't many people who pass through." The idea that Oliver would have seen a carrier pigeon crossed Evelyn's mind, but then she remembered that he had not actually seen the scroll attached to the pigeon.

Evelyn was distracted from the mystery by laughter floating up from the ground. With his leather boots swishing through the bluebells and ferns, Pip was running toward the berry patch. His strawberry-blond hair looked more strawberry than usual from being drenched in the river, and his clothes were splattered with water as well. "Were you trying to hide? I can see you both up there!"

Birdie made a good-natured reply, and Evelyn replaced the partially carved piece of wood where she had found it. She descended carefully to the ground, resolving to mention it to Nora later.

Each of the baskets was filled after only a few more minutes of picking, and the three still had enough energy left to race back to the cottage, taking care not to spill a single berry.

Nora was pleased to see their harvest and had all her jam-making equipment laid out. "I'll tell you a story while we sort the leaves and stems out from these blackberries," Nora offered. "It has to do with growing things, in fact."

Perched on rush-seated stools, the three

children looked up at her expectantly. Nora continued, "Years before I was born, a family was traveling through the countryside, looking for a place to build a home and start a farm. Much of the town they were from had burned in a mighty fire, and they wanted to start again. Eventually, they came to a place that seemed to be perfect. There was a village near a beautiful lake with welcoming people and rich soil. A plot of land was available nearby, so the family bought it and started to set up a farm. In their fields they planted wheat, corn, and oats, hoping to discover what grew best in their soil, but none of what they planted grew above the height of their knees. The next year, they planted fruit trees of all sorts and berry bushes on half of their farm. On the other half they tried to grow vegetables. But the trees and bushes died too, and the vegetables yielded barely enough for the family to eat."

"How disappointing!" Pip commented.

Nora nodded in agreement. "For the third year, though, the family decided to try something totally different. The mother and father loved flowers, and they decided that they would fill their entire field with hydrangeas, peonies, hollyhocks, daffodils, roses, and every other type of flower they could find. They enriched the soil and sought advice from their neighbors. And to the astonishment of all, their magnificent garden thrived where none of the other crops had. People came from villages nearby to marvel at the huge, colorful collection of blossoms."

Rosie had come into the kitchen and stood behind the children, listening carefully. "That would indeed be wonderful to see."

"Did they do anything with all those flowers, besides admire them, of course?" Evelyn asked.

"They did," Nora continued. "It was a lot of

work to figure out the right times to plant bulbs and seeds for all the different flowers since each type of flower has its particular time of year to bloom, but they kept their flower farm going and would carefully pack crates of flowers in soft, wet moss and mail them all over the kingdom. They became quite renowned at the time for the unique flowers in their bouquets. And the family came up with recipes that used the flowers, too. In fact, that's where I got my love of rose jam. My grandmother and grandfather were the people in the story, and I grew up visiting their home and beautiful fields of flowers often."

"I love that story!" Birdie exclaimed. Pip and Evelyn nodded enthusiastically in agreement. "I hope you tell us another story about your family sometime. Thank you," she said to Nora.

Evelyn flicked an insect away from her gleaming berries and gathered up a few that had rolled away from her pile. "I wish you had heard Aunt Nora tell some of the ancient legends of the kingdom that she's been teaching me on our walks to the village," she told Birdie. "She is such an amazing storyteller!"

"You have some exciting stories of your own to tell," Nora pointed out with a smile.

"Yes. In fact, there is a legend right here in Bluebell Forest, though I don't know what it is."

Pip looked up, and Birdie questioned, "How do you know about it, then?"

"Do you remember when I said I had found a carrier pigeon?" Evelyn asked. The siblings nodded. "Well, part of the message on it said that Bluebell Forest is the forest in some legend. Even though I've lived here all my life, I've never heard of this supposed legend. So someone knows a story about this area that I don't, and I hope I can one day find out what it is."

Birdie and Pip gazed at each other with wide

eyes. “Someone else knows about the legend of this forest!” Pip blurted out. Then he clamped his hand over his mouth, alarmed. Rosie looked up, her attention caught.

Evelyn was shocked by Pip’s words. “Do *you* know a legend about this forest, Pip?” she urged.

The boy looked at her, wide-eyed and unsure. His mother hurried over before anyone could say anything. “Pip always tells the truth,” Rosie interjected. “He does know a legend, at least part of it. It’s simple, really. It’s a tale that the second ruler of this kingdom hid something in this forest—that’s all.”

“That’s all!” cried Evelyn, completely astonished. “But no one knows anything about the second ruler of this kingdom. Heartsong has no records going back that far! Where did you hear this?”

Nervously, Rosie glanced from side to side.

Folding her arms, Nora came over to stand by her. Kindly yet firmly, she said, "Rosie, I think you are withholding information from us. We are your friends, but we can't help and support you if we don't know the truth. Why are you really here?"

CHAPTER 14

To everyone's surprise, Rosie readily agreed. "I will tell you what I know about the legend and how," she said. "I'll be right back." Rosie quickly walked down the hallway and disappeared into her room.

The two siblings looked at each other in wonder. "She's never shown it to anyone outside the family before," Birdie said quietly to Pip.

What is she looking for? wondered Evelyn. Her family had items of their own that were precious, but none of them were secret.

A moment later, Rosie returned with a brittle

yellowed scroll, which she held gingerly in one hand. Across the bottom the parchment was ragged, as if part of it had been torn off. "Here it is," Rosie said. Fingering the scroll gently, she explained, "I have half the legend. It was handed down from generation to generation in our family. My children have known about it ever since they were old enough to read, and we've always been intrigued by it."

I am, too! Evelyn thought. *But why would Rosie's family have brought this with them? Have they had to leave their home permanently? People don't usually carry delicate heirlooms with them on their travels.*

"Normally we keep this protected in a special desk drawer with a lock and a hidden compartment," Rosie continued, as if reading Evelyn's thoughts, "but we decided that it was important enough to take it with us when we embarked on our journey. I'll read it to you."

She took a deep breath and unrolled the scroll with care. "From King Hugh, second ruler of Heartsong Kingdom: When the time comes that the sister kingdoms threaten to disunite, go to the forest where bluebells blossom abundantly in the Valley of Willow Lake. Here lies Laughing Pipes Mill, where I have hidden the pipes that will reveal the true history of this land and the way to unify the kingdoms again. You must not seek the pipes until then. They are hidden well. You will find them—"

Rosie looked up. "The rest is missing. For as long as anyone in our family line can remember, this scroll has been torn."

Evelyn had been leaning forward to catch every word, but she rocked back abruptly at this news. "So you came here to find the pipes?" she asked in awe.

Rosie nodded. "Yes, and I'm sorry. Perhaps it would have been best to be up front. We have not told you any lies, and we don't want to be dishonest. None of us have poked around anywhere."

"You have been the best of guests," Nora assured her. "You have nothing to feel bad about."

"Thank you. Before we told you about this, we wanted to get to know you first and see if we could trust you," Rosie continued. "And we do. But now that you know, would you be willing to help—"

Before Rosie could say any more, a knock sounded at the front of the house. Evelyn was a little disappointed that Rosie's explanation was interrupted, but she went to open the door, expecting to find a bakery customer. When she saw the friend who stood there, she was filled with gladness.

"Welcome, Russell!" Evelyn exclaimed. "What brings you here?"

The kind neighbor looked anxious, and Evelyn could sense that something was amiss. "A letter for you came through the post office, and I also brought a newspaper from the inn. I thought you might want to see it," Russell said.

Taking the proffered papers, Evelyn asked, "Which should I read first?"

"Maybe you had better read the newspaper before the letter so we know what's going on," Nora suggested.

Trembling with unknown worry, Evelyn nodded. She began reading aloud: "According to all sources, Heartwood Kingdom has just shut off its border with Heartsong. No one is allowed in, and no one is allowed out, including the many Heartsong citizens who were there on business. No information has come regarding these trapped visitors either, since letters are not permitted to pass through the closed border."

Nora seemed struck almost speechless, but she mustered her voice to ask, "Is that all?"

Shaking her head, Evelyn replied, "No. There's one more thing." She looked down at the paper and read, "Also, for the first time, the news has broken that the king and queen of Heartsong Kingdom and their two children have gone missing. No one has seen them for two weeks."

Reeling from the news, Rosie gasped. "This means my husband cannot come back for us."

Evelyn and Nora looked at each other, slowly locking eyes. "My family is probably there, too," Evelyn realized.

Birdie looked like she was about to cry. She asked in a shaky voice, "How long will it be?" No one opened their mouth to answer. No one knew.

Concerned, Evelyn gazed down at the sealed letter she still held in her hands. Even though she knew Mama needed to go to Heartwood for treatment and hoped her family had crossed over the border before it closed, a tiny part of her wished they had somehow gotten stuck on the Heartsong side and would come home soon. Maybe they had been delayed or discovered a doctor who could help in their own kingdom. A tiny flicker of hope lit up inside of her. Yes, the letter had taken a little longer than expected to arrive. Perhaps they were delayed.

Ripping open the letter, Evelyn hardly dared to look. And then she suddenly scanned it, taking in all the information at once. Her stomach sank with finality as she read the letter aloud. "Dear Evelyn, We are glad to tell you we have just gotten over the border and are headed to the doctor. Once we arrive, we will send more news. How is the bakery faring? We're sure you and Nora have it running excellently, but if you run into any trouble, let us know. We think of you constantly and can't wait to be home with you. Love, Mama and Papa." Evelyn bit her lip, knowing that no more letters would be coming over the border for a very long time.

At the bottom of the page, there was an addition written in large, whimsically shaped letters. "Dear Evelyn, I wish you were a bird and could fly to us in Heartwood. I love you. Your sister, Alicia." The six-year-old's message made Evelyn smile, but tears pricked at her eyes, too.

Her family had made it in time and would be able to get Mama to the doctor she needed. It should have been good news. But they were trapped in Heartwood.

CHAPTER 15

Wanting to be alone for a little while, Evelyn went outside. She needed some quiet time to contemplate all she had recently learned and to pray. From the birds hiding and flitting about in the sunlit forest came an alluring chorus, and the sound of the river gently lapping against the sand wove its way through the trees to the cottage. Right now, though, Evelyn felt drawn to the well-used, ancient mill.

As she entered, her footsteps stirred up the debris that had lain untouched since the millstone had broken, and the light from outside illuminated countless specks of dust swirling in the air. In a corner, Evelyn knelt on a pile of empty grain sacks and began a quiet prayer.

"Father in Heaven, please help me know what to do. The people I love most dearly are stranded in Heartwood, and they can't come home until the kingdoms come together and open the border to each other." Evelyn paused, awed. That sounded like an impossible thing to accomplish . . . except for the fact that she, of all people, had access to Laughing Pipes Mill, the place that, according to the legend, would reveal how to unify the kingdoms. *There is definitely something in the mill. I've never heard of the Valley of Willow Lake, but this has to be the right place since the plaque said Laughing Pipes Mill.* She continued her prayer. "If there is anything that will help the kingdoms, please help me find it. And please keep my family safe."

Evelyn rose from the stack of burlap sacks. Though she wasn't sure the best way to start searching for the pipes or how she would know when she found them, she began walking around the perimeter of the room, feeling for any cracks in the walls that could house a concealed compartment. *There aren't even that many places to hide something*, Evelyn thought, *but if the pipes were anywhere obvious, they would have been found by now.*

As she focused closely on the walls, Evelyn was startled to hear a creak from the entrance to the mill. She spun around. At the threshold stood Oliver, his clothes rumpled, his usually tidy hair disheveled, and a look of deep concern on his face. Leaning heavily on his shoulder was a girl who appeared to be a couple of years older than Oliver, perhaps twenty. She bore a remarkable resemblance to him and was obviously ill.

"Please, my sister needs help," Oliver beseeched Evelyn, his voice quiet yet urgent with concern.

"Of course," Evelyn said, her heart longing to ease the girl's suffering. "Come into the house. I'll get Nora."

Hastening across the yard, Evelyn went to find her aunt. Nora stood in the kitchen, rinsing a pile of rose petals she was preparing to use in a recipe.

"Oliver and his sister are here," Evelyn announced quietly, "and she looks quite ill."

"Where are they?" asked Nora without hesitation, not even appearing startled at the information that Oliver had a sister. "I'll do all I can to take care of them."

"I invited them in, but they're waiting in the yard still."

With her efficient, brisk walk, Nora followed Evelyn out to the front step. When Nora saw the bedraggled girl shivering in the warmth of the summer afternoon, concern filled her expression. "What is your name?" Nora asked as she approached Oliver's sister.

It was obvious to Evelyn that the girl didn't want to give out more information than she had to. Looking from Nora to Evelyn, she finally responded, "I'm Bridget." Her voice was hoarse with illness.

Nora gently held the back of her hand to the girl's forehead, testing her temperature. "You definitely have a fever," she said. "You must lie down right away so you can rest and get better. Come with me. The bedroom at the end of the hallway will be the quietest. Evelyn, get some extra blankets and the box of medicines from my room."

The four formed a procession into the house. Evelyn hastened to the large wooden chest in the living room that was normally used as a place to sit but also held linens and blankets. Using all her strength to lift the heavy lid, she at last was able to prop it open and pull out two thick, soft quilts.

"Here, I can carry those," Oliver said from behind her, taking the bulky blankets from her arms. He had already helped Bridget to the room Nora had offered.

"Thank you," she replied gratefully with a quick nod, turning to hurry across the hall.

When Evelyn opened the door to Nora's room, the first thing she noticed were the ferrets. But she could see only four of them. *Where is Freddy?* she wondered.

In a hurry, Evelyn pushed the ferret out of her mind as she searched around the room for the medicine chest.

She saw a wooden box on a shelf. *That must be it*, Evelyn thought, but as she reached upward, something caught her eye. Six feet above the ground, a long, squirming ferret clung to the curtains.

"Freddy!" exclaimed Evelyn. "What is going on?" While she was wondering if she should try to get the ferret down to safety and how to reach him, Freddy scampered halfway down the curtain with ease. He turned to face Evelyn and revealed a mischievous look, as if he were taunting her, then bounded up to the top of the curtain again.

Evelyn laughed. "Okay, Freddy. You've proved your point. Don't worry, I won't attempt to make you come down." Then she took the box from the shelf, unlatched the small brass closure, and opened the lid to make sure this really was the medicine chest. When she looked inside, she was left with no doubt. One half was packed with many square glass bottles that were filled with different herbs. The other half held tweezers and small vials of colorful liquids as well as cloudlike cotton balls and rolls of bandages. *How exciting it would be to learn to use all of these!* thought Evelyn. She had learned some things about treating animals from a nearby farmer, but she hoped someday she would receive formal training and become a real veterinarian.

Right now it was a person who needed help, though. Evelyn hastily closed the box before she headed down the hall and knocked softly on the door of the far bedroom. Nora appeared at the door. "Thank you," she said, taking the box.

Evelyn went to wait in the living room with Oliver, who was wringing his hands worriedly. "I wish I had known what Bridget needed. I should have found a doctor or someone to help sooner," he said.

"Everything will work out, I'm sure," Evelyn soothed. "Aunt Nora has told me she's very experienced in nursing people, and she will know just what to do."

Talking quietly together, Evelyn and Oliver waited for Nora, who emerged from the room at the end of the hall a little while later and washed her hands. Finally Nora came over to them.

Anxiously, Oliver asked, "Will Bridget be all right?"

Nora nodded. "Thankfully, the fever is mild, so I think your sister will recover without complications. I need to know where you're living, though, so I can tell your parents."

Looking uncomfortable, the boy fidgeted. "Well, we've been camping in the forest," Oliver admitted, "and neither of my parents are anywhere nearby."

"What do you mean?" asked Nora incredulously. "I need the truth, and the whole truth. You can trust us," she said firmly. "You knew that this was Laughing Pipes Mill long ago, and no one else in this valley knows this. We need to know what is going on, and we will help you."

"I will tell you if you promise not to tell anyone what I say."

From his leather satchel, Oliver slowly pulled out a scroll—with the top ripped off. "It's the legend of Bluebell Forest. Well, at least half of it," he said.

Heart beating fast, Evelyn gasped. "Where did you get that?"

"It was handed down through our family," he said proudly.

"Why would your family have that?" Evelyn asked.

Oliver took a deep breath and spoke confidently. "Because my father is the king."

Check out these other Level 5 books from The Good and the Beautiful!

Violet and the Volcanoes: The Mysterious Manor
By Amy Drorbaugh

Violet and the Volcanoes: Alone in Iceland
By Amy Drorbaugh

1.0NSP526-163385 Printed in USA Dec-2025